To
Jaime

1999 is The YEAR!

Samuel
6/99

# WEALTH STARTS AT HOME

## 15 Secrets That Could Make You a Fortune

**DAVID D'ARCANGELO**

McGraw-Hill

New York   San Francisco   Washington, D.C.   Auckland   Bogotá
Caracas   Lisbon   London   Madrid   Mexico City   Milan
Montreal   New Delhi   San Juan   Singapore
Sydney   Tokyo   Toronto

**Library of Congress Cataloging-in-Publication Data**

D'Arcangelo, David.
    Wealth starts at home : 15 secrets that could make you a
fortune / David D'Arcangelo.
      p.  cm.
    Includes index.
    ISBN  0-7863-1128-2

    1. Finance, Personal.  I. Title.
HG179.D355   1997
332.024 dc—21                96-40001

# McGraw-Hill

*A Division of The McGraw·Hill Companies*

1 2 3 4 5 6 7 8 9 0  DO DO 9 0 9 8 7 6

ISBN 0-7863-1128-2

*Printed and bound by R. R. Donnelley & Sons Company.*

McGraw-Hill books are available at special quantity discounts to use as premiums and sales
promotions, or for use in corporate training programs. For more information, please write to the
Director of Special Sales, McGraw-Hill, 11 West 19th Street, New York, NY 10011. Or contact
your local bookstore.

*This book is dedicated to the people. May this be the jolt, the dynamite, the explosion, or the massive inspiration you need to take your life to the level you truly dream of and deserve. My goal is to provide you with the facts, figures, and vital information you need to relieve the financial pressure and live a life of total abundance free of financial worry.*

*This book would not have been possible without the unyielding belief system instilled in me early on by my parents and grandparents, and my carousing brothers, Michael, John, and Tom. To my lovely wife, Carrie, who is both my partner and advisor. I'm blessed to have you and your belief in me.*

*Sports seemed to teach me "never say never"; to friends like Billy Mullen, Clark Crowley, Jake and Jay, Jack and Jonathan, Alfred and Bernie, and all the others who allowed me to take that attitude and parley it into a business career. To Mike Brienzo, who showed me the possibilities, Randy Perkins who pointed me in the right direction, and Anthony Robbins who opened up my mind so I could see the big picture.*

*Special thanks to my wonderful assistant, Leslie Viviani, and to a host of others for their help in providing support material that is included in this book; you'll see their names referenced throughout.*

*Special thanks to McGraw-Hill, who made this book possible, and my publisher, Caroline Carney, who not only caught the big vision and future of the home-based business movement, but actually came to our first meeting having already reworked my original outline for the book into a clear and concise game plan to help make this book a major bestseller.*

# C O N T E N T S

# Introduction: Financial Freedom Begins at Home

In this book I've collected 15 of the best-kept financial secrets that could guarantee you a fortune upon retirement. I'll share them with you one by one and give you suggestions on how to make the most of the opportunities you have. You already may be familiar with some of the ideas, but others will be totally new to you. Regardless, by systematically working your way through the strategies I've suggested, you can create a pathway for you and your family to build financial security. Finally, I'll prove that you can create wealth 300 percent faster by building a part- or full-time business and working out of your home. Combine these proven home-based business wealth-building principles and immediately implement the 15 best-kept financial secrets for the investment of your new money and you could create exponential growth and discover total financial freedom.

Something has happened to the American dream. Once upon a time, not so long ago, the rules were simple: Work hard, save your money, and you'll be a success. Today, hard work and common decency don't seem to be enough. The rich get richer (not withstanding the burden of astronomical taxation), the poor get poorer (despite government "help"), and the middle class is slowly being squeezed out of existence. Clearly, we have a new "F" word for the nineties and beyond: *Freedom.*

In the coming years, will you be one of the *haves* or one of the *have nots?* When was the last time you felt financial pressure? Are you getting fed up with the impossibility of making it financially in today's society? You're not alone. Now, as never before, Americans are crying out for business income opportunities. What I have witnessed firsthand, in my extensive travel throughout the country, is that people are desperately seeking that one phenomenal opportunity that will allow them to genuinely take control of their lives. At every level of society, people are becoming disenchanted, frustrated, and just plain mad. They have the right to be! They've had it up to here with working harder and harder for fewer rewards . . . watching helplessly as bigger and bigger bites are taken out of their paychecks to pay colossal government debts. If you have experienced any of these feelings; if you have reached (or are about to reach) your peak years of productivity; if you're beginning to feel you'll never fulfill your potential in your current career or get paid what you're really worth; if you know deep in your gut that somehow you should get more for your efforts—then this book is for you.

Just reflect on these major magazine stories.

- "Will Technology Wipe Out Jobs for Good?" (Friday, July 28, 1995, *USA Today,* Money Section)
- "The Bloodletting at AT&T Is Just the Beginning—The Telecom Industry Must Ax 100,000 More Jobs Over 5 Years" (*Business Week,* January 15, 1996)
- "Corporate Killers—Wall Street Loves Layoffs. But the Public Is Scared as Hell. Is There a Better Way?" (February 26, 1996, *Newsweek*)
- "How to Earn $100,000 Working at Home—Close to 2 Million Americans Make 6 Figures at Home and So Can You" (March 1996, *Money Magazine*)

It doesn't take a genius to see that society is changing at an unprecedented rate. Technological breakthroughs promise a wealth of new freedoms and opportunities. At the same time, many of our cultural institutions are being redefined and we can no longer count on the same old standbys to carry us through. Here are just a few of the examples of the financial expectations that we grew up with that are going the way of the dinosaur.

- **Unlike our parents and grandparents, few of us will spend our entire work life employed by the same company.** Instead, we're experiencing corporate downsizing (or what I call "capsizing"). I foresee that by the year 2000, the average person will be switching from a solo career to multiple sources of income (MSI). We've all heard about the sweeping layoffs by corporate giants like IBM and General Motors. AT&T has shed over 125,000 workers over the last 11 years alone. In a recent note, it has announced another 30,000-plus person layoff over the ensuing years. AT&T's 302,000 employees have all known that their jobs are on shaky ground since Chairman Robert E. Allen announced on September 20, 1995, that by 1997, the company will split into three companies—telecommunications equipment, communications services, and computers.[1] And, according to a May 1994 issue of *Business Week,* there were 192,572 layoffs in the first quarter of 1994 alone—an average of over 3,106 job cuts from American corporations every day! In other words, folks, you're on your own, and welcome to the 21st Century.

- **Social Security is a ludicrous joke.** The October 9, 1995, issue of *Forbes* called it "The Legal Ponzi Scheme." *Forbes* writer Reba Koselka goes into detail as to why she believes younger Americans have come to understand that for them Social Security isn't a benefit, it's just another tax. She writes: "If the U.S. Government were required to keep its books the way businesses are required to keep theirs, the national debt wouldn't be $5 trillion. It would be about $17 trillion, an amount equal to about 2½ times the national gross domestic product. That $12 trillion difference is the estimated obligation of the government for its unfunded pension liabilities under Social Security."

  The system that once funded our parents' retirement went bankrupt a long time ago, and there's no way we'll be repaid more than a token (if that!) of what we contribute to Uncle Sam from every hard-earned paycheck. Broken promise after broken promise will leave every American working longer as the starting date for those eligible for Social Security is delayed for future generations. The fact is that, with a broken Social Security system, we will be forced to bail out Social Security at our own expense.

- **Government is encroaching on our livelihood more relentlessly than ever before.** Besides Social Security taxes, we

1. Catherine Arnst, "For a Pink Slip—Press 2," *Business Week,* November 27, 1995,

pay withholding taxes, disability taxes, property taxes, and luxury taxes. At one point, the government even tried snack taxes in the state of California. You name it, and chances are we pay tax on it! This doesn't end when you die, either. Your heirs will have to pay up to 55 percent estate tax, which is the cost levied by the government just to leave this life! What's more, the battle for control between the government and the voters is likely to continue into the future. It seems that everywhere you turn, more and more hands are eagerly digging into your pockets and telling you what you can and cannot keep.

## SOCIAL INSECURITY

It's been said that if the Social Security program were a private enterprise, those who've run it into the ground would be thrown in jail.

Unless you take aggressive measures to provide for your own retirement, you're playing by the old rules—and they're not set up for you to win. You may have noticed that the Social Security system as we know it is completely overburdened and that those counting on government paychecks to fund their "golden years" are in for a rude awakening. In fact, the situation is likely to get even worse for retirees, as a bill now pending before the legislature (as of January 1995) would raise the eligibility age and could reduce allotments.

Who came up with the magic age of 65 for retirement, anyway? President Roosevelt did, back in the 1930s. Why? Because at the time, *most Americans were dead by age 64*. FDR was no fool; he helped design a system that wouldn't have to pay anyone except a very small percentage of people who lived past age 65. However, retirees are now living well into their seventies, eighties, and beyond, and Social Security is collapsing under the strain.

## POWER TO THE PEOPLE

Are you in control of the flow of money in your life and are you satisfied with the direction it seems to be headed? Look at the people you spend your time with, like co-workers and friends. Are they satisfied with their financial lives, with the places they've been, and where they're going?

How about your parents? As much as you love your family and friends, are they living the lives of their dreams—the lives you know they deserve?

Over the years, I've observed something that's true for the vast majority of us: Despite playing by the rules and doing everything "right," many of us just aren't headed where we want to be financially. We don't feel in control of our lives. We're already struggling to catch up, trapped in jobs where the best we can hope for are yearly incremental raises that don't keep up with inflation. Some of us are 40 or 50 years old and don't seem to have any better financial future than when we were 30. We're set up to become just another statistic when we join the 94 percent of the population who end up either dead or *dead broke* by age 65.

Let's face it: Most people just don't know how to take control of their finances. Nor do they understand how to profit from the changes that are reshaping society. The average person has been conditioned to think like an employee/consumer (someone who parts with her time for a salary or wages or dollars for a product or service). But if there's one quality that is needed for success in the coming decades, it's the mindset of an *entrepreneur.*

**Entrepreneurs are those who strike out on their own, committed to creating financial freedom by taking total control of their work environment and income goals.** Rather than accepting the conditions of a corporate lifestyle (where other people tell them how much they can earn, when they can expect to receive a raise, and what career track they should follow), entrepreneurs *take the risks to get the rewards.*

## SWITCH TO RIGHT-BRAIN THINKING

During the last 200 years, the majority of people were paid to use the left side of their brain—that's the computer side of the brain, which adds, types reports, pushes buttons, answers phones, runs a jackhammer, paints houses, works as a laborer, holds a management position, sells goods and services, and so on. These are all duplicable and replaceable functions that put you at the mercy of your employer because your position can be easily learned by someone else (as hard as that may be for you to imagine). During the next 10 years as well as the next 30 years, each of us has the opportunity to leverage his mind and get paid what he is really worth, utilizing the right side of the brain. That's the creative side of the brain, where everyone possesses the entrepreneurial skills necessary to design the future of his or her choice.

Change can be uncomfortable, but you must learn to deal with it head-on if you're ever to secure any measure of financial freedom for yourself and your loved ones. One of my mentors once told me, "Where there is chaos, David, there will be opportunity—and you must have the vision to see the opportunity." It's a lesson I've never forgotten and one from which I've profited handsomely over the years. It has compelled me to develop a pretty sharp mental "radar" so I can seek out the hidden opportunities that other people are either too lazy or too timid to take advantage of.

It doesn't take a lot to start using this system yourself—just a little bit more initiative than the next guy. But if you accept the challenge I'm about to present to you, it can make all the difference as to whether you end up with the 94 percent who live with regret and broken dreams . . . or with the 6 percent who have a genuine golden future ahead of them.

## LEARN TO THINK LIKE THE HOUSE

No one has yet found the goose that lays the golden egg or the tree that sprouts dollar bills—or at least, if they have, they're not talking. So if you're planning to get rich quick, then good luck . . . because you'll surely need it. The world is full of so-called opportunities where you are told you can bypass the necessary sweat, tears, and due diligence and go directly to Park Place, pass Go, and collect $200. Of course the most accurate term for this type of "opportunity" is *gambling*—let's call a spade a spade! If you're playing for the sake of playing, and if you have a pretty clear idea of how rare it is for someone to beat the odds, that's one thing. But people who allow themselves to be convinced that they can profit without taking any responsibility or doing any of the work are living in a fool's paradise. These are the people whose dollars end up financing all of the luxurious upgrades to every plush casino along the Las Vegas strip. Every time a gambler plunks down his chips at the blackjack table, he's betting against the house—*and the house wins 99 times out of 100.* Sucker bets are fine for some people, but are they good enough for you?

My mission is to be your advocate, to open your eyes, to share with you the knowledge, principles, and strategies that will enable you to separate yourself from the 95 percent or so of the population—the gambling employee/consumers—and join the less than 5 percent of the population, the entrepreneurs who think like the house. (If this sounds an awful lot like the retirement percentages, where 94 percent of retirees end up broke and only 6 percent live in comfort, it's no coincidence!) No matter what your current position—whether you're earning a starting salary or a six-figure income—if you want to get better results and start taking more active control of your future, you've got to learn to evaluate financial opportunities in a new way.

## THE WINNING HAND

It doesn't take a lot of money to start a collaborative marketing or a direct-selling venture or other form of home-based business. However, it does require that you make a clear, committed decision to developing the three elements of a winning hand: *entrepreneurship, savvy,* and *conviction.* Once you have these on your side, the rest is easy. In this book, I'll show you how to drive your income to new levels using a home-based business—and if you don't have any money at all to start off with, then I'll show you how to get some. My point is simple and powerful: *Anyone can achieve financial freedom by leveraging his or her mind, creating an additional profit center out of the home, and applying a few basic tax-reduction and investment strategies.*

Now that you've been introduced to the benefits of entrepreneurship, let's briefly cover the other two elements of a winning hand. The first is savvy, which means educating yourself in the basics and developing an overabundance of common sense.[2] For example, explore informed trade sources, like *Entrepreneur Magazine, Success Magazine, Black Enterprise,* and *Money Magazine.* I'm not suggesting that you need to cram every possible detail into your head or take everything onto your own shoulders. In addition to exploring these resources, you'll want to locate a reliable business resource with a proven track record. Having the right technical help on your side will be a critical element in increasing your chances for success.

Once you find one or two experienced and attentive home-business resources, you can help them help you by knowing what you want to achieve. In my corporate consulting business, I much prefer informed clients to passive ones. In fact, I push everyone I work with to become more knowledgeable and involved. *The bottom line is: No one cares more about your future or your money than you do!* The best clients are those

---

2. Throughout this book I've provided an excellent list of products, services, magazines, and references, to help you turn ideas into action and profit.

who don't panic or waffle; they are certain about their predetermined objectives and, by understanding the rules of the game and adapting for their own needs the single strategies I give them, they are much more likely to experience success at a faster rate. They use my research and advice as valuable input, but not as the final word. My clients always make the final decision—and why shouldn't they? After all, if you are unable or unwilling to decide what is in your own best interest, then who should take on that responsibility instead? More precisely, no one cares as much about *what* and *who* you're protecting as you do, and no one else has the same *emotional investment* and hopes, dreams, and desires as you do. That brings us to the third element of a winning hand, which is *conviction.*

## THE ANATOMY OF CONVICTION

Conviction is the unshakable belief that you're doing it right. It is solid sense that you've made the best possible decision given all the facts available to you at the time. Conviction is not for wimps who constantly second-guess themselves or are too cautious to go out on a limb. Nor is it for "leap first, look later" types who pull foolhardy stunts in order to prove something. It's true that there is a simple element of risk that is automatically thrust upon anyone who plays the game of finances. By the same token, there is a world of difference between a smart, calculated risk, and a dumb, no-win risk. A large part of what I'll do in this book is point out the different types of risks to help you determine your smartest course of action (and obviously I'm convinced that owning your own home-based business is the smartest risk you could ever take!). The better you learn to differentiate between a dumb risk and a smart risk and to identify the wise choices for yourself, the better you'll be at *thinking like the house.* This mind-set enables you to quickly size up a situation and identify the consumer (who is being sold) versus the house (who is doing the selling). Once you understand these dynamics, you can make a decision that's in *your* best interests.

In Las Vegas there are casinos that advertise a 95 percent payout on slot machines. Sound like great odds? For the house, it's an absolute gold mine! A fraction of 1 percent of gamblers will make a lot of money, a small percent will make a little, and the vast percent will be lucky to break even. But the house unfailingly gets a 5 percent return on *your* money. For every $1 you drop into a slot machine, the house averages 5 cents, thank you very much. When you add up all the house's small advantages over the long haul, you begin to get an idea of how profitable the gaming business is. In 1994, the public wagered $330 billion dollars—and the gaming industry netted $30 billion in revenue after all was said and done. How much do you think the gamblers took home?

Here's the bottom line: Whenever you're considering whether to buy something, such as a business, a new TV, or blue chip stock, take a few moments to consider it critically. In other words, *look at it in a different way than the way in which it has been presented to you.*

## QUESTIONS TO HELP YOU THINK LIKE THE HOUSE

1. How can I get close to the customer?
2. How can I turn my customer into a business partner?
3. What's in it for the customer? What's in it for me?
4. Who's really set up to win here? Is this transaction ultimately to my benefit?
5. What is my *"unique selling proposition"* of why people will buy from me?
6. Am I giving customers more value than they are paying for?
7. What's my "best case scenario"? What's my "worst case scenario"?

Ask yourself the questions in in the accompanying box whenever it seems even remotely appropriate, and pretty soon it will become automatic to your way of thinking. Here's an example of how I went into this critical thinking mode the last time I bought a car. As I was signing the papers, my trusty salesperson decided to let me in on a "great deal—credit life insurance. If you've ever financed a major purchase such as an automobile, boat, or large appliance, then you've probably been offered the same set-up. For an additional monthly sum, you're assured that if you pass away, the policy will pay the company back and you'll owe nothing on the product. In my case, the salesperson told me it would cost me only an additional $20–$30 a month to guarantee the payoff of the loan should I pass away prematurely.

Obviously, credit life insurance is a great opportunity—for the car dealership. "Look," I told my trusty car salesperson, "I'll tell you what. If

I die, you can keep the car. I don't think I'll need it any longer. As a matter of fact, I think it would probably be a good idea for you and all the other folks on the sales force to pool your money together and purchase credit life insurance on *me,* not the other way around!" If I had bought the credit life insurance, my best case scenario would have been to have died the next day, thus getting my "money's worth" on the policy—some best case!

Is it really all that different in the standard life insurance game? When you buy a whole life policy, universal life policy, or variable life policy, what you're really doing is betting against the life insurance company. You're betting that you'll die young, while the insurance company is taking a calculated risk that you'll stick around long enough to pay into a policy over an extended period of time, say 30 years or more. In the meantime, the insurance company generally gets to invest your money and make the spread on the difference between what it pays you and what it earns on the investment, plus fees.

Are you starting to get the picture? Whoever sets themselves up as the house gets to keep all the chips, or at least most of them. The consumer gets strung out, accumulating a chip here or a chip there, *enough to keep him playing the game.*

When making any decision, then, reevaluate the situation from the other person's perspective, identify who's likely to gain the most, and figure out who's doing the paying . . . and who's doing the playing.

So let's get started! If you've decided that you're tired of being limited by other people's ideas of how much money you should make . . . if you're fed up with giving the best of your attributes and abilities every day without getting paid anywhere near what you're really worth . . . if you believe in yourself and the future in spite of the turbulent years ahead . . . and if you have the guts to set a goal, the stamina and drive to do whatever is necessary to achieve it, and the vision and passion to know that financial freedom is within your grasp—then stick with me. Together we'll rediscover the American dream, as we explore how you simply can't afford not to be your own boss and own your own home-based business.

## DO YOU HAVE WHAT IT TAKES TO BE AN ENTREPRENEUR?
### (answer yes or no)

**1.** Is it unacceptable for you to be paid below what you are really worth? Yes - No

**2.** Are you interested in a part-time business to replace/compliment your current income? Yes - No

**3.** Are you willing to sacrifice your personal time to build long-term financial freedom? Yes - No

**4.** Can you generally make good decisions based on sound information? Yes - No

**5.** Do people consider you to be honest and a person of integrity? Yes - No

**6.** Do people (generally) seriously consider what you have to say? Yes - No

**7.** Do you consider yourself coachable by others? Yes - No

**8.** Are you the type of person that can go the distance in the pursuit of your long-term objectives? Yes - No

**9.** When things go wrong, do you accept the responsibility versus blaming others? Yes - No

**10.** Will you work hard for something you really believe in? Yes - No

**11.** Do you enjoy sharing what you truly believe in with others? Yes - No

**12.** Would you like to take greater control of how you live your life, both financially and professionally? Yes - No

*Check your answers. They may surprise you. If you answered yes to 10 or more of the 12 questions, you're on your way to entrepreneurial success. If you answered yes to 6 to 9 questions, you have your work cut out for you. If you answered no to more than 5 questions, you should find a partner to strengthen your weaknesses and your motivation, because without a partner you don't stand a chance.*

# Strategy #1: Get Free Money for Your Home-Based Business

## USE YOUR WITS, LIVE YOUR DREAMS, AND BEAT THE SYSTEM

Whether you realize it or not, you're living in one of the most exciting times of our country's history, a period that will prove to be the turning point for the livelihood and fortunes of millions of Americans. Currently, up to 37 million people—one-third of the entire U.S. population—are conducting full- or part-time businesses out of the home, representing a 20-fold increase over the last 10 years. What's more, this number is expected to grow at least 15 percent annually, which means that by the year 2000, in the United States alone, roughly 90 million people—*one out of every three persons you meet on the street*—will be involved in some form of home-based business. Think about it: in the next five years, up to 90 million individuals will have made the monumental decision to be their own bosses, work in the comfort of their homes, and pursue their dreams. This is the greatest mass movement of people in the shortest period of time entering this unstoppable new era in over 200 years, since the industrial revolution.

I have two vital questions that will help you determine your future. *First, what is the product or service you will buy, sell, or represent in this new marketplace?* And, if you're not already thinking about your answer, then here's my second vitally important question: *Is the world changing faster than you are?* If you're not being paid what you're really worth right now, how many more weeks, months, or years will it take before you finally decide that life is passing you by?

If the system won't recognize you for your true talents, then only one person can—you! *You must take control and put yourself in the way of opportunity.* If you've previously been cut out of the mainstream for any reason whatsoever, perhaps because you are a woman, a member of an ethnic minority, or because you simply are not taken seriously, then this message is especially potent:

> Success does not discriminate—only people can do that—and sometimes we do it against ourselves.

The greatest form of discrimination has nothing to do with race, color, or creed but has everything to do with ourselves standing in our own way with outdated, risk-inhibiting references holding us back. You need to "get in the way of opportunity" so that when it presents itself, you can seize it—grab it by the throat, if you have to—and build on it like nobody's business.

I've written this book not only to guide you in making the most of your money but also to share with you my simplest, most powerful strategies for maximizing your own attributes and abilities. No matter what your financial condition, regardless of where you're starting or what resources you have, there is one type of investment that is always the best you can possibly make: *an investment in yourself.* This means finding a way to set it up so that your livelihood—the work you spend one-third or more of your life doing—is as rewarding as it can be, on every possible level, from mental to emotional and from financial to spiritual. If you can't enjoy the benefits of being able to set your own income and lifestyle goals, then it's a sure bet that whatever you're doing to earn a living is actually "costing" too much!

The brave new world is no longer looming on the horizon; it's here. We're moving into an era of global business, about to experience a period of exponential growth the likes of which hasn't been seen since the end of World War II. The fall of the Iron Curtain has opened up new markets and cultures eager to join the international community of commerce. In 1996, President Clinton signed the sweeping Telecommunications Act, ending government rules that have maintained barriers between local and long distance calling, cable TV, broadcasting, and wireless services. As you read this, the United States is crossing the threshold on a bold journey that has never been undertaken by any other nation in the world and has set the tone for the 21st century communications industry. With one stroke of the pen, the entrepreneurial floodgates have opened wide to this trillion-dollar industry, allowing every would-be entrepreneur—from the one-person home-based business to the 300,000-person megacorporation —to compete for a share of the prize money. There are 5.5 billion people on this planet, and the opportunities for expanded trade are mind-boggling. With a shift from military defense spending to high-tech research and development and scientific applications, America's industrial base is going through significant restructuring. Fueled by a change in people and government, the democracy of everyday people (you and I) is dismantling the delusion of a centrally controlled business system. With some exciting developments that continue to take place, in the most forward-thinking megacorporations, the *real action* will explode in smaller arenas throughout the country—anywhere talented individuals or dedicated groups have a great idea that they're willing to implement. Now as never before the business opportunities for people of any education and any background seem almost limitless.

It has become increasingly clear that a revolution is taking place in the way that wealth is created in this country. It's called "small business" and it represents the wave of the future. Ninety-five percent of the job growth in America in the last three to four years has been in small business (i.e., any enterprise employing one to four people). Woman-owned small businesses, in particular, are creating more new jobs than any other employer today, including big business; in 1992 alone, woman-owned businesses increased by 32 percent.

## CREATE A VIRTUAL COMPANY

Certainly one of the most rewarding aspects of a home-based business is the earning potential it represents. Research shows that where the average employee makes an annual salary of $26,000, *the average home-based business household earns $50,250 a year.* Of these households, figures indicate that 20 percent earn over $75,000 per year, and 66 percent are owned by women! Without a doubt, entrepreneurs are dramatically changing the face of corporate America.

In 1994, the international director of Young Entrepreneurs con-

## THE FEMININE FORCE

According to *Work Force 90's,* "women will make up a projected 37 percent of the workforce by the year 2005 and are currently starting businesses at twice the rate of men (as reported by *Working Woman Magazine*).
In the book *Mega Trends for Women,* it is noted that from 1980 to 1989,
the number of U.S. entrepreneurs increased 64 percent overall, while the
number of female entrepreneurs grew 96 percent. During the same period,
U.S. entrepreneurial revenue grew 69 percent overall, while the revenue of
female entrepreneurs grew 145 percent. In fact, the National Foundation of
Woman Business Owners reports 4.5 million women own their own business."

"According to the labor department, more than 50 percent of the American workplace is made of minorities and women, yet it appears that their
advancement is hindered by artificial barriers. The time has come to tear
down the 'glass ceiling,' and many people are accomplishing this through
self-employment. Even though change for women is slow in corporate
America, they have become a major force in the financial world. In a report from Syracuse University, women own about 75 percent of America's
stocks and bonds; 65 percent of the savings accounts; own or control 70
percent of America's capital; and own 85 percent of the consumer buying
power. Ready or not, women are changing the face of America."

ducted a random survey of male and female Bostonians aged 18–30 that
revealed a typical disillusionment with the corporate track. Top-ranking
items on the survey's "corporate hit list" were office politics, stifling su-
periors, inflexible work schedules, killer commutes, low pay, and pressure
to conform to a daily grind. It's small wonder that owning one's own business is an increasingly attractive alternative to the nine-to-five treadmill.
Besides, now there are more technological resources than ever before to
support home-based operations: computers, modems, faxes, and cellular
phones, to name just a few.

Home-based business is the entrepreneurial opportunity that all of
America is looking for. If you want a career in an industry that is one of
the highest paid in the country . . . if you want to start a business that pays
you what you're really worth . . . then you have the soul of an entrepreneur.

April 1 is April Fools Day.
April 15 is Tax Day.
To many investors,
there's not much difference.

This is a recent quote I read from an advertisement by the international and private banking house J. P. Morgan. The fact is, if you expect to have any money in your life, you must study money.

How would you like to learn:

- How anyone can tap into the $426 billion dollar industry that will triple in 5 years.
- How to be aboard a cruise around the Hawaiian Islands with your loved one on February 1 at the government's expense.
- How to pay for your children's college education and wedding costs with tax-free money.
- How to amass a $1 million family fortune with totally tax-free and tax-deferred money.
- How to pay your children $4,000 or more, totally tax-free, every year.

Remember, the workforce is divided up between entrepreneurs and employees. The employee has made a decision and a commitment to build someone else's dreams and, as an entrepreneur, you've made the vital decision to build your own dreams. The first step in your journey is to identify the enormous money-making benefits provided by your own government, to give you every possible chance for success during your initial start-up phase and throughout your entire business career.

## HOW ABOUT A $3,300 TO $15,000 RAISE?

The following strategies can put an additional $3,300 to $15,000 cash in the pocket of every home-based business owner, depending on her level of work and investment every single year. Those numbers quintuple to $16,000 to $75,000 over a five-year period of time—an amount you cannot afford to do without. The biggest challenge that we all face is that no one ever taught us the rules to the game of money. I'll shatter your belief systems of what you have been taught about money and home-based business and literally accelerate the quantity and quality of your life from this day forward.

The best way for me to do this is to share with you the simple story of a friend of mine in South Florida who was always complaining about paying too much in taxes; never having enough money for his family or to put toward his children's education; or even having enough money to take his wife out to dinner and take the vacation that they truly deserved.

Have you ever noticed that the people closest to you, such as your family and friends, seem to discount your advice the most? My friend Jerry had a full-time job and was also a great lover of bass fishing. I had been telling Jerry about home-based business and how it could put more money back into his pockets and literally eliminate the financial frustration that was beginning to have an effect on his family, his relationships, his business, and his health. As we continued to talk and get together over a three-year period of time, Jerry gave me every reason imaginable why he couldn't start a home-based business. I'll admit that some of them were even good excuses. Finally, I put an ad in the South Florida newspaper that read as follows:

---

**JERRY THE BASSMAN**
All The Best Spots
*$150 a day*
**World Class Fisherman**
(123) 123-1234

---

Just ask yourself: When was the last time you felt financial pressure? What has been the financial decision-making process you've used up to this point in your life? If you keep making financial decisions the way you've been making them, what will your life look like 10, 20, 30, or even 40 years from now? Just imagine how your decisions could affect your family, your relationships, your business, and your health.

## TAKING ACTION

I explained to Jerry that if he kept doing what he was doing, his family would literally retire at the poverty level. Now keep in mind, Jerry was extremely happy with his job but just couldn't seem to cover all of his expenses. He'd continually run out of money before the end of the month. The last 10 days of each month, he would be filled with such anxiety that you could see the negative impact on his attitude. The first day that the ad ran in the paper, Jerry began receiving phone calls and immediately called me to find out if I had actually placed the ad in the paper. I admitted I had and told him that not only would he take these fine people fishing but that he was to charge them $150 a day and give them $300 worth of value.

This ensured Jerry's future success by encouraging more referral business back to his company. It also helped him develop his USP (Unique Selling Proposition). Every person who starts a business or currently owns a business needs to have a unique selling proposition. Your USP is the absolute bottom-line reason why individuals should do business with you versus any of your competitors. In Jerry's case, he built such a powerful USP that before long everybody knew that fishing with Jerry provided a more exciting, fascinating, and successful fishing trip than any other organization in the Florida Keys. Jerry's boat was noted as being the most up-to-date and comfortable of any comparable boat. Jerry's expertise and wisdom garnered from his 30 years of experience aided by his gregarious and fun-loving personality put every angler at ease, encouraged hope, and delivered results.

With his telephone, answering machine, and a spare room with one desk and a chair, Jerry started a home-based business, employing his wife, Linda, and his two children. He built an additional profit center, maximized tax benefits, and began to accumulate a $1 million totally tax-deferred and tax-free family fortune at the ripe old age of 40.

Jerry's business is destined to succeed for three reasons: (1) Jerry developed a simple outbound marketing and follow-up plan; (2) realizing his business shortcomings, Jerry hired his spouse to manage the day-to-day business; and (3) Jerry kept expenses low, maximized tax benefits, and created cash flow almost immediately.

Of the almost three million recorded businesses that are started every year, nearly 24 percent close within two years. The difference between those that succeed and those that fail is that most people spend more time shopping for a washing machine that costs $400 than they do planning a business strategy for their career. The answers to questions concerning potential market, competitors, pricing, cash flow, marketing, and so on, all play a major role in their success. In this book, you'll learn why providing home business opportunities to 90 million people is the greatest market of all time and how government tax benefits will subsidize your business until you're so successful you have no choice but to pay taxes.

This is how Jerry did it:

**1. Turning personal assets into tax deductions.** Jerry took his boat, which he had already bought, and paid for it completely. The Internal Revenue Service (IRS) says that you can take previously owned assets and move them into your business and write them off at the lower of cost or market value, utilizing the depreciation schedules. Jerry's boat when purchased new cost $35,000 but at its current age has a market value of $20,000. Using the IRS depreciation schedules, Jerry will be able to take a depreciation deduction of $3,060 for his first year in business, a $4,900 deduction for his second year, and a deduction that declines thereafter based on the IRS tables. If Jerry uses the boat 50 percent of the time for business, then he gets 50 percent of these numbers. In other words, he multiplies the percentage of business use of his boat for the entire year by the annual depreciation allowance to come up with his total depreciation allowance.

**2. The tax deductible automobile.** Jerry also began deducting the pickup truck that he uses to pull the boat as a business expense. I sat down and helped Jerry calculate whether he should take the actual cents per mile deduction or the 31¢ per mile IRS standard deduction.[1] The IRS gives you both options. You obviously want to use the method that provides you with the biggest deductions. Based on Jerry driving 22,000 miles annually for business, we figured out the following:

**Method A:   Actual Cents per Mile Method**

| | |
|---|---|
| Total deductions | |
| (Includes auto expenses except interest) | $7,920 |
| Business miles (annually) | 22,000 |
| Total cents per mile ($7,920 ÷ 22,000 = 36¢) | 36¢ |

**Method B:   Deductions Using IRS Standard Rates**

| | |
|---|---|
| Cents per mile | 31¢ |
| Business miles (annually) | 22,000 |
| Total deductions (31¢ × 22,000 = $6,820) | $6,820 |

In this case, you can see that Jerry's pickup truck drives 22,000 miles per year on business to bring him a tax deduction of $6,820 using the IRS's standard rate of 31¢ per mile. However, under the actual

---

1. In 1996, the IRS standard mileage rate is 31¢ per mile. This number is subject to change annually.

method, this deduction comes to $7,920—a method that provides him with a $1,100 advantage over the IRS method.

If you choose the IRS standard mileage rate, you cannot deduct actual operating expenses, such as depreciation, maintenance and repairs, gasoline (including gasoline taxes), oil, insurance, or parking and vehicle registration fees, among others. If you want to use this method, you must choose it the first year you put the vehicle in service. You can switch to the actual method at a later date if you start out with the IRS standard rate, but only if you use straight-line depreciation.

**3. Additional benefits.** Now most of the gas, equipment, and supplies for Jerry's business fishing trips are totally tax deductible in the year that he purchased them. In other words, Jerry is doing what he loves to do and the government is subsidizing his business with tax deductions on every business purchase. In the first year alone his total of $2,500 expenses was totally tax deductible.

**4. The tax deductible home office.** Utilizing the storage space in his garage for the various fishing equipment and supplies, as well as sectioning off the spare bedroom in his home, Jerry now utilizes the home office exemption to deduct 20 percent of the expenses of running his home. This includes 20 percent of the utility bills, home insurance, roof repair, and house cleaning. In the first year alone, he will have $5,632 in home office deductions, which will provide a tax refund of approximately $2,285.

If you don't have an extra bedroom to section off for your home business, do not be concerned. You can also use a portion of a room either in your home or in an apartment (that you do not own), although you must abide by the IRS regulations and use that area exclusively and regularly for your business. Exclusive means just what it says, only for business, and regularly means on a continuing basis. Occasional or incidental business use of a part of your home or apartment does not meet the regular use test even if that part is used for no other purpose.

**5. Hire your spouse.** All Jerry needed to start his business was a desk, a chair, a separate business phone line, and a $46 answering machine. It was as simple as placing an ad, setting up appointments, and going fishing. The problem was that after three months, when I called Jerry to ask him how the business was going, he replied with a resounding, "Outstanding!" And he continued to answer "Outstanding!" to every question after that. I quickly sensed that Jerry had an administrative disaster on his hands. The bottom line was that after three months of having a great time fishing, Jerry hadn't billed anybody. So immediately we took Linda,

Jerry's wife, and brought her into the business. Jerry and Linda purchased a small computer so they could not only track business and expenses but also develop a mailing list of prospective clients and corporate accounts. The mailing list is invaluable for repeat business. Linda not only took more professional control of the business and freed Jerry up to do what he does best, but she also generated a direct mail campaign to corporations with Jerry acting as a fishing guide for salespeople who had won sales contests. At the same time, she went to a list service and purchased, for one time use, 2,000 names of prospective fishermen who had bought fishing products in the past. Linda did a direct mail campaign and generated 70 responses with a "free offer" and booked 30 additional fishing trips at the new price of $250 each, thus creating an additional $7,500 in income.

     **6. Pay your children tax-free money.** With two children, 8 and 10 years old, Jerry and Linda are continually buying school clothes, sneakers, baseball gloves, and movie tickets, as well as sending their kids to camp once per year. They also are looking at $50,000 to $100,000 per child for college expenses as well as wedding costs. In order to reduce these costs, Jerry and Linda both utilize the personal exemption for each member of the family that they support, which provides a dependency exemption of $2,550 (subject to change annually) per year for each child. At the same time, by placing their children into the business and paying them a fair and reasonable wage, their children become a tax deduction. The children are assigned simple projects such as washing the boats, stuffing envelopes, cleaning the vehicles, and even keying data into the computer. Based on a tax court decision (to which the IRS agreed), you generally can hire children as early as age seven. If you are unincorporated and you hire your own children, who are under 18 years old, there is no Social Security and Federal Unemployment tax. You simply deduct the salary as an expense, and the employee claims the standard deduction of $4,000 tax free.

     You then set up a custodial account at a mutual fund company that will accept minors and you put the tax-free money away each year for each child. You invest the money and act as the custodian of the children for their benefit. Even if the children are over 18 years old, they will most likely be taxed in a lower tax bracket of 15 percent versus your 28 percent, 31 percent, 36 percent, or 39 percent bracket. If you're in the 36 percent bracket and your child is in the 15 percent bracket, you still come out 21 percent ahead.

     **7. Tax deductible health insurance.** You can write off 100 percent of health insurance using a little known strategy called "family employment." Since 1954, the IRS has allowed you to hire your spouse or chil-

---

## SUCCESS MADE SIMPLE
## $100 Monthly Equals a $3 Million Personal Fortune

If you think this strategy is child's play, just listen to my reasoning: You pay a child $100 per month and 20 years later those dollars have grown to $90,000 invested at a reasonable rate of return. The children are now in college and you let them live off the interest for additional spending money, which at 8 percent would generate $7,200 per year of fun money.

At 25 years old, you turn the account over to your child and tell her if she continues to fund this account at $100 per month assuming the same reasonable rate of return, at age 55 she will have a $3 million personal fortune.

---

dren or to incorporate if you have neither and write off 100 percent of your health insurance premiums. In this case, Linda, as an employee, went out and bought health insurance, which Jerry, as the owner of the business, then expensed to the corporation and reimbursed Linda without Linda having to pay taxes on that income. Linda elects the family coverage for health insurance and thereby covers Jerry, her husband, as well as the children and it's 100 percent tax deductible.

As a sole proprietor, which means you pull your chair up to your desk, get into the business to make a profit, have a plan in place, and devote time to making that plan profitable, you may qualify for deductions not only on insurance premiums, but also vision care, dental and uninsured medical, tax-deductible life insurance (up to $50,000), disability income insurance premiums, chiropractic care, hospital bills, laboratory fees, orthodontics, and examinations. Let's assume Jerry and Linda made $50,000 this year and they have $5,000 in medical insurance, expenses, and deductibles. What are the tax benefits?

### What You Could Save Beginning Today

| Taxable income | Medical insurance, expenses, and deductibles | Multiplier[a] |
|---|---|---|
| $40,101–$96,900 | $5,000 | 47% |

Your Tax Savings Total:   $5,000 × 47% = $2,350[b]
*Total family medical insurance, expenses, and deductibles*

Notes:

[a] Actual savings may vary per individual. Assumes an average state tax rate of 4 percent and a FICA rate of 15.3 percent, earning $50,000.

[b] This illustration assumes an average state tax rate of 4 percent and a FICA rate of 15.3 percent when calculating the multiplier. Actual savings may vary.

These strategies and benefits are but the tip of the iceberg, providing both tax-deductible business benefits plus the most effective tax-free and tax-deferred money machine ever created. As you continue to work your full-time job, open your eyes to the enormous opportunities that are available for the self-employed. The IRS will literally subsidize you in your business with tax benefits until you're so successful you have no choice but to pay taxes after you've used up all the benefits. At the same time, you've now encountered a vehicle that will allow you to literally stop throwing a portion (up to 50 percent) of your paycheck away in taxes and put that money where it truly belongs, in your investment account.

In the accompanying table you'll see an example of Jerry and Linda's home business deductions. In the first year, they claimed 15 percent use of the home plus some purchases for furniture and office equipment and were surprised to receive $5,632 in home office deductions, giving them a tax refund of $2,255. Add to that Jerry's use of his vehicle driven 7,000 miles at 31¢[2] per mile (using the IRS standard mileage rate), a tax deduction of $2,170, and an additional refund of $1,134—for a to-

## You Can't Afford Not to Be Your Own Boss

| Deduction | Total | Home Office % | Home Office Deduction | Tax Benefit Rate | Tax Refund |
|-----------|-------|---------------|-----------------------|------------------|------------|
| Mortgage interest | $10,000 | 15% | $1,500 | 13.02[a] | $ 195 |
| Property taxes | 1,650 | 15% | 247 | 13.02 | 32 |
| Utilities | 1,600 | 15% | 240 | 52.3[b] | 124 |
| Home insurance | 500 | 15% | 75 | 52.3 | 39 |
| Roof repair | 900 | 15% | 135 | 52.3 | 70 |
| House cleaner | 1,200 | 15% | 180 | 52.3 | 94 |
| Depreciate home | 1,700 | 15% | 255 | 52.3 | 133 |
| Furniture | 2,500 | 100% | 2,500 | 52.3 | 1,307 |
| Office supplies | 500 | 100% | 500 | 52.3 | 261 |
|  | $20,550 |  | $5,632 |  | $2,255 |

Summary

| | |
|---|---|
| Tax refund home office | $ 2,255 |
| Tax refund business mileage | + $ 1,134[c] |
| 1st year | $ 3,389 |
| Five years of tax refunds | $16,945 |

Notes:

[a] Self-employment tax rate.

[b] Self-employment tax rate of 13.02 percent, plus 31 percent federal tax, plus 8.3 percent state tax.

[c] Assumes you drive 7,000 miles in business and use the IRS 31¢ per mile deduction.

---

2. This is the IRS standard deduction for 1996, which is subject to change annually.

tal first year tax refund of $3,389 ($16,945 over five years). Remember, this is the home office and auto deduction only.

Your thoughts may determine what you want in life, but your actions will determine what you get. The concepts and strategies I've discussed are but the beginning of the journey into a whole new strategy of creating wealth in America. This new strategy drives every individual back home and helps you turn your home into an outrageously successful money machine. If knowledge is power, then your power lies in feeding your mind the facts, figures, and information necessary so you can maximize every dollar you receive in the most tax-advantaged manner possible. It's no wonder that people you know who start their careers at age 20 might become one of the following statistics at age 65:

- 20 percent don't survive.
- 39 percent have annual incomes under $10,000.
- 24 percent have annual incomes between $10,000 to $19,999.
- 14 percent have annual incomes between $20,000 and $49,000.
- 3 percent have annual incomes over $50,000.[3]

The paradox we all face in the world's richest nation is that many people live in unnecessary poverty . . . where will *you* be? Paying up to 50 percent of your income in taxes and sin taxes and then having to live off the remaining 50 percent is a prescription for poverty. It's nearly impossible to take the remaining 50 percent of your income and try to pay your insurance, mortgage or rent, auto expenses, general living expenses, clothing expenses, children's current education expenses, transportation expenses, utility bills, and so on, while at the same time trying to put away money for investments, cash reserves, children's future education, retirement plans, and the vacations you truly deserve. That's why it's an absolute *must* that you become a master of your own destiny and begin implementing these strategies that will help you reach your true financial potential.

---

3. National Center for Health Statistics, *Monthly Vital Statistics Report* 40, no. 13 (September 30, 1992), Table 6. Income and poverty data for the year 1991 are from: U.S. Bureau of the Census, Current Population Report, Series 1–60, no. 180, "Money Income of Households, Families, and Persons in the United States: 1991," Table 6, August 1992. There can be no assurance that this trend will continue for people entering the workforce today.

# Strategy #2: Multiple Sources of Income (MSI)

A series of predetermined moves from project to project, crisscrossing industries and employers. Starting out with one full-time job and developing two or more projects on a part-time basis to maximize income and talent. Creating wealth up to 300 percent faster, multiple sources of income (MSI) entrepreneurs fret little over what they can't control and refocus on the three ingredients over which they have absolute control: time, effort, and MSI.

## MSI MEANS EQUAL OPPORTUNITY

Sometimes even the obvious is the most impossible to understand. I travel throughout North America conducting financial seminars. Most of these programs have been specifically designed to share the metaphors and financial strategies that will shatter your belief system and change how you were taught to think about money and investing. These philosophies and metaphors, many of which you'll find in this book, will increase your level of financial understanding. The amazing thing to me is that, after my seminars, a large portion of the audience often come to me and tell me that they loved the financial strategies. Then these members of the audience almost always ask the question, "Where do I get more money to implement such fantastic financial strategies?" Driven by the need to achieve total financial freedom in our lives, most of us have absolutely no idea whatsoever what to do to earn additional money to implement those strategies. After four years, it became increasingly clear to me that more people were asking me where to get the money rather than asking me how to implement the strategies.

## THE SEARCH IS ON

At this point it became self-evident to me that, along with everything that I was studying in the newspapers about technology, downsizing, and the move to home-based business, I had literally been test marketing these concepts over the previous four years. I immediately began to switch gears and have dedicated the last two years of my life to searching for the finest home-based business opportunities in North America today. Now this is a bold task in itself, considering that the franchise business is a $758 billion industry, home business is a $426 billion industry, and a huge number of small businesses start up every single year. I recognize, as well as you do, that nobody has time to go out and read every magazine that promotes hundreds of home-based business opportunities when the average person hardly has the time to review one business opportunity effectively. People want bottom-line facts and figures reduced to a simple, understandable format. Once their interest is aroused and they've checked out the initial facts, they can then take their journey to the next level and research to their heart's content.

The result of all of my years of analysis is that I finally came up with the six hottest industries for home-based businesses in North America that fulfill the needs of the beginner, the intermediate, or the advanced entrepreneur. The monumental task was to uncover opportunities that would provide anyone with the greatest percentage chance of success in the first 24 months of business.

These are businesses that anybody can get into and the majority of which provide an income the first month without creating enormous overhead. These are businesses with consumer-driven products that will literally save or make you money beginning from the first day you get involved. These are businesses with necessary products and services so that people don't have to justify spending additional dollars every month. Have you ever received a service or bought a product that you were so excited about that it absolutely, positively did more than you ever imagined it would and, in fact, you got more value than you even paid for? Wouldn't this be an incredible product to sell to other people? That's exactly the criteria I used for my multiple sources of income (MSI) business qualifiers. Pay close attention and I will describe the six most advantageous and lucrative MSI industries for the next five years.

## The Six Hottest Industries

**1. A $1 Trillion Industry by the Year 2000.** The global information superhighway . . . long distance phone service . . . the Internet . . . the World Wide Web . . . wireless communications . . . personal communication services. . . .

These fast-paced, high-tech words describe a revolution taking place in the $1 trillion telecommunications industry. Beginning with the 1984 AT&T/Bell breakup, over 600 new telecommunications companies have been established. Efficient equipment, computerization, new long distance services, and now the deregulation of the local phone service will allow every individual to reap the financial rewards of the telecommunications revolution. The world is shrinking at an exponential rate driven by the speed of telecommunications and technology.

You can reap the financial rewards of this revolution by putting yourself in between buyer and seller and setting up your own tollbooth on the information highway. Currently, AT&T, MCI, and Sprint make up almost 90 percent of the entire long distance service in the United States alone. In the new era of competition and deregulation, we now are seeing retailers in the marketplace that give the home-based business opportunist the potential to represent or undercut the big three long distance providers with reseller discounts and competitive pricing that could save the average individual anywhere from 10 to 50 percent on his long distance phone bills alone. Driven by competitive pricing, excellent customer service, and a $200 billion worldwide long distance business, you'd be able to offer customers: residential and commercial long distance service at a lower cost; crystal clear fiber optics; flat rate prices; 800 number services for home and office; paging; calling cards; Internet access; digital television; and risk-free guarantees. This is the business where the middleman can squarely set up his tollbooth between the buyer and the seller. Without any inventory or any purchases to deliver, you can begin collecting long-term residual income with a ground floor opportunity that is both low risk and highly profitable.

By starting your own home-based business in the fastest growing industry in the world—*that has never had a down quarter in its entire history*—you will now be able to develop a long-term residual income that requires:

- No capital investment.
- No products to purchase.
- No inventory to sell.
- No delivery of any products.
- No collections.

- No quotas.
- No employees.
- No customer risk.
- No experience needed.

Direct selling organizations have moved in and filled the void after deregulation provided network marketing direct selling opportunities producing unprecedented income opportunities in a business growing at exponential rates. You make money in two ways: (1) getting customers and (2) getting customer-getters (i.e., other people who would like to be in their own business). These companies will pay you a percentage of the long-distance charges every month for each person you sign up. There are no monthly quotas and you get paid for every one of your long distance customers. It's free to be a customer.

When you are gathering customers you'll interest others who would like to participate in the home-based business telecommunications industry just like yourself. Many of these companies have set aside dollars so that you can sign up these individuals to be in business within your organization. You may also make additional money just for training them and giving them the greatest chance to be successful. Bonuses are paid when you bring in new distributors and when those distributors sign up as few as three customers (which may include their own service). These bonuses can be as high as $100 and it is not unheard of for individuals getting in the business to make anywhere from $300 to $1,000 their first full month in the business.

The companies with the larger vision are interested not just in selling long distance services, but also providing a full line of diversified products in the telecommunications industry. These products may include not only long distance service but also pagers, calling cards, calling stickers, digital satellite television, and Internet access. The companies with true vision will continue to expand this product mix to include all forms of products that will be tied to the telecommunications industry. As this industry continues to evolve through the deregulation of local phone service, we will look for these companies to become a player in the local marketplace and the newly deregulated utility industry. In fact, I think the most exciting exponential growth will come in the next three to five years when these companies may be adding highly competitive utility rates to their product mix and selling them to the same installed customer base. To understand the magnitude of this growth you must first come to understand that the average long distance bill per household in the United States is approximately $30. When you add local service that these companies may be offering in the future, add an additional $6, and utility bills in three to four years add an additional $60. You have now taken a $30 monthly bill for which each home-based business distributor receives an override and literally tripled that bill to over $90 per month. In other words, on the same installed base of customers, the representative, in three to four years, may have the potential to triple his or her income. If we speculate that Congress will approve these companies to sell their services along with local service just like they are selling long distance, the future potential income may be staggering. Clearly the power is in owning the distribution system and this industry has figured out how to do it with independent direct selling distributors who all pay their own expenses. They offer cheaper rates on a variety of services on products the public is using every day, every week, every month, and every year.

Selling people something they are already paying for and now offering them a discount is the equivalent of going to the checkout line at the supermarket with your basket of goods. Sign a new customer form and immediately you begin receiving a 10 percent to 40 percent discount on your bill.

How much to get started: $50–$750

Who to contact: The Direct Selling Association (202) 293-5760

**2. Passport to Success.** With the deregulation similar to the onslaught of the telecommunications industry, opportunities are changing the entire landscape of the travel industry.

The aftermath of airline deregulation in 1978 has opened the doors to fierce competition within the travel industry. With the convergence of the travel industry rapidly approaching $4 trillion in 1996 and on track to become the number one industry in the United States by the year 2000, it has become increasingly clear that millions of aspiring home-based business entrepreneurs may choose travel as their business or may choose to participate on a part-time basis and enjoy the travel benefits.

The travel industry now opens up to these individuals not only to be independent travel agents, but also to capitalize on the tremendous benefits available to independent travel agents while they also hold other full-time careers or home businesses. In other words, independent travel agents may also become an industry unto itself supporting corporations and individuals holding down other careers.

The problem with the industry is that travel has been grossly under-promoted operating in an environment with high advertising costs. Hotel vacancy rates soar as high as 50 percent in various locations and many airlines fly with available seats during nonpeak seasons. The bottom line is that resorts need publicity, airlines need seats filled, and hotel vacancy rates must be absorbed. The solution: the education and training of independent travel agents to promote the exciting world of travel. The direct selling industry has stepped squarely through into this enormous opportunity presented by travel and transferred the marketing costs down to the independent distributors promoting travel at their own expense.

Traditional travel agents have to attend travel school costing up to $5,000. At the same time, opening an agency, like any other small business, can cost from $50,000 to $100,000 only to find our eager travel owner trapped behind a computer doing clerical work and shuffling papers without any hope of seeing the blue waters of the resorts they not so long ago dreamed of visiting. The inflexible and undesirable work schedule of the traditional travel agent puts them in a position operating under the old 80/20 rule where 80 percent of the revenue is generated by 20 percent of the people working 50- to 80-hour workweeks.

Independent travel agents working out of their homes have no complicated paperwork and devote a majority of their time to promoting travel which is why they got into the business in the first place. They can work in the comfort and security of their own homes, be their own bosses, work their own hours, and have complete access to the exclusive benefits available only to travel agents.

---

### FIVE WAYS TO GET PAID

- Get commissions paid back on your own travel.
- Earn commissions on the travel of everyone you refer.
- Generate commission for referring each new agent.
- Earn overrides on all the new agents you refer and all the travel they book.
- Double your rewards with incentives, bonuses, and even auto allowances.

---

For as little as $495 independent agents receive the travel industry educational program and their travel agent identification credentials. When booking travel they simply call or fax their itinerary to the main office. Many companies now have online computer software that allows independent agents to go online with their associated company and search for the most competitive rates and vacation packages available. Itineraries and tickets are issued directly to the client and the process is easy, convenient, and profitable.

Independent agents now have up to five streams of income. For those that select network marketing (direct-selling distribution), they will also earn commission for enrolling and training other agents, and receive organizational commissions, bonuses, and overrides. Travel commissions, resale profits, wholesale overrides, car bonuses based on production, profit sharing, and even leadership bonuses are the rewards independent travel programs will use to generate the greatest exposure and sale of travel in the industry today.

Perhaps being able to travel at bargain rates appeals to you, or maybe you desire to build an incredible business that can lead to your financial freedom! Home-based business travel is the wave of the future and will speed the growth of travel and tourism as the number one industry throughout the world by the year 2000. Supported by tremendous industry tutorial training, high-tech reservation centers, weekly live conference calls to promote training and enrolling, weekly/monthly business briefings, company-sponsored regional training, fax-on-demand, computer reservations systems, and a distributor support system where people are motivated to support other agents in their business, the travel industry has created one of the most exciting second income business opportunities that will allow the masses to travel the world at a fraction of the cost.

- *Travel and tourism* will create 144 million new jobs by 2005.
- *Travel and tourism* is the world's leading economic contributor, producing an incredible 10.2 percent of the world gross national product.
- *Travel and tourism* is the leading producer of tax revenues at $655 billion.
- *Travel and tourism* is the world's largest industry in terms of gross output, approaching $4 trillion in 1995.
- *Travel and tourism* accounts for 10.9 percent of all consumer spending, 10.7 percent of all capital investments, and 6.9 percent of all government spending.
- *Travel and tourism* employment from 1990 to 1993 grew 50 percent faster than world employment.

With the advent of computer technology and online services, the joint venture relationships of major airlines, cruise lines, package providers, and independent agents will bring a fresh new profit center to what used to be considered a personal or business expense.

How much to get started:   $250–$499

Who to contact:   The Direct Selling Association, (202) 293-5760

**3. Billions In Nutrition.** In excess of 250 million Americans and 6 billion people worldwide—up from 1.5 billion only 100 years ago—continue the lifelong pursuit of the fountain of youth. Industry sales of vitamins and mineral supplements exceed $4 billion annually and show no signs of letting up. The proliferation of scientific research, biotechnology, and the insatiable appetite of the "feel-good" public promise to catapult this industry into the hundreds of millions of dollars range on an annual basis.

Clearly, more than 50 percent of the US population feel we can't get the right mix of vitamins and minerals to keep us healthy due to our hectic schedules. Public awareness is being heightened by a continued stream of new releases touting the benefits of breakthrough products that will not only enhance our mental capabilities but also make our hair grow, add muscle tone, brighten our smiles, widen our arteries, increase our sexual prowess, and extend our life span.

Since the United States government released the recommended daily allowances (RDA) for vitamins in 1940, the nutrition industry has transformed itself into one of the most profitable markets in the free world. With 75 million baby boomers in the United States alone and a senior marketplace that constitutes the largest percentage age group on a year-to-year basis, nutritional products are poised to bring diet and nutrition into the 21st century. Researchers continue to formulate optimal nutrition products that promise to add 5 to 10 years to our life span. Products that offset the aging cycle and repair damaged cells because of excessive consumption or exposure to toxic substances continue to put this industry at the forefront of the public's mind. Products such as amino acids and peptides, minerals, trace elements, and vitamins all add to the list of non-natural substances that will help improve our anti-aging properties.

An entirely new product category titled "alternative medicine" will play a significant role in this multibillion dollar industry. Americans currently spend in excess of $15 billion on alternative medicines, ranging from herbal products, treatments, and medicines to chiropractic care. Approximately two-thirds of the products in this category—$10 billion—is paid in out-of-pocket cash.

The human body contains over 400 muscles, 206 bones, 403 major joints, 300 sweat glands, 14 billion nerve cells, 100 trillion other cells, and over 60,000 miles of lymph and blood vessels that are continually bombarded with over 400 pesticides currently licensed for use on American foods. Over 2.5 billion pounds of pesticides are sprayed on our crops and our land that directly and negatively attack our body function and retard performance over long periods of time.

The direct selling industry eliminates hundreds of millions of dollars in marketing and distribution expenses by bringing products directly to the marketplace by network marketing associations and direct selling organizations that provide better one-on-one consumer-oriented education and sales. More products are coming to market in the categories of nutrition and alternative medicine through the network marketing and direct-selling distribution channels within the next 5 years than we've seen in the last 50 years. Add to that the fact that industry-related products and services that are sold generally are taken regularly and that these consumers often purchase additional products and services. Add new product value along with residual income to an existing multibillion dollar industry and you have one of the top industries for the decade ahead.

How much to get started:    $50–$500

Who to contact:    The Direct Selling Association, (202) 293-5760

**4. The Global Satellite Mall.** Satellite Television, Success Programming, Products—you won't find these companies in the *TV Guide!* You won't stumble onto this channel while you're surfing the 500 channels on your TV set! And just when you thought there was nothing worth watching on your TV . . . along comes a satellite network and company dedicated to helping you develop your own personal programming utilizing the many services and materials at its disposal. The rules for success have always been the same: If you want to earn more—you have to learn more and the fastest and most effective way to learn in America is to plug in to education and information in the comfort of your own home.

The television networks you are familiar with—NBC, FOX, and MTV, for example—are supported by advertising. So, their primary influence and financial support come from their advertisers. Even the Public Broadcasting System (PBS) is supported by government funding, viewer donations, and corporate sponsorships.

One company, on the other hand, has created a new paradigm. They do not ask for donations, and will not sell out its message to advertisers. Instead, they ask that their subscribers redirect a small portion of the dollars they are currently spending monthly to support the network.

Subscribers purchase products from the company's global mall catalog. This is a unique catalog featuring hundreds of specially selected products including essential household items, *New York Times* bestsellers, pharmaceutical-grade health and wellness products, music, and much more. By doing this, viewers support the company's mission and programming, while at the same time, benefiting from two major trends.

- Home shopping
- Buying direct from manufacturers at wholesale prices

The company takes a portion of the profits from the sale of these products and uses it to support the network. The company also uses these profits to create a financial opportunity that is unlimited. Affiliates are paid for expanding the network and for promoting the unique products that flow through it. Rewards can include substantial bonuses, commissions, and overrides, as well as long-term, on-going income.

What a way for a television network to support its viewers—life-skills programming beamed into subscribers' homes, direct wholesale buying from manufacturers, and a reward system that allows individuals to earn while they learn.

It's no wonder *The Wall Street Journal* said that few observers of the self-help movement are betting against the company.

## The Mission

Why do some rise to greatness and others barely scrape by? Clearly, access to the right information was an important element. People also need a positive, life-enhancing environment, conducive to growth.

Out of a genuine desire to help others, this company envisioned an enterprise where positive, motivated people could come together and embark on a never-ending quest to develop the best qualities within. They know that excited, dynamic people like to be around similar individuals. And they understood the need for a financial reward system that would motivate everyone to achieve.

**The stars come out every night . . . and every day too.** The programming features some of the world's greatest success coaches: Brian Tracy, Les Brown, Denise Austin, Mark Victor Hansen, Bruce Jenner, Jim

Rohn, Gladys Knight, Dr. Bernie Siegel, Fran Tarkenton, Art Williams, just to name a few. The topics covered are as varied as the interest of successful people today—family and parenting, relationships, career and business, health and wellness, sales and negotiating skills, personal finance, success and motivation, and much more. The ideas and strategies showcased would normally cost you thousands of dollars monthly. The programming channels may include:

- Children's programming
- Multiple language broadcasting
- Corporate training

- Continuing education
- Home schooling
- Closed captioning for the hearing impaired

How much to get started:    $199–$495
Who to contact:    The Direct Selling Association, (202) 293-5760

**5. The $25 Million Opportunity.** With a divorce rate of 50 percent and climbing, one lawsuit for every three Americans, three trial court cases filed every second in America, and 54 percent of all Americans in a legal situation or about to enter into one—do you think there might be a need for national legal services? A new industry has evolved taking advantage of the fact that legal problems cause the average American to seek legal advice about five times per year, according to an American Bar Association survey. An estimated 85 percent of all consumers' legal inquiries can be answered over the phone in seven minutes.

---

- *Barron's* **National Business Weekly writes:** *"Pre-paid legal services will REVOLUTIONIZE the legal profession. IT'S THE WAVE OF THE FUTURE . . ."*

- **USA Today writes:** *"Legal aid could be (the) top benefit: THE PLANS MAKE IT POSSIBLE FOR PEOPLE TO USE LAWYERS where they wouldn't ordinarily (because of cost)."*

- *The Wall Street Journal* **writes:** *"There's Legal Aid for the poor (and) private attorneys for the rich, but UNTIL NOW we've NEVER had anything for the working middle class. THANKS TO PRE-PAID LEGAL PLANS, this group is FINALLY able to AFFORD legal services."*

- **The American Prepaid Legal Services Institute says:** *"IT'S A WONDERFUL IDEA. Prepaid coverage makes legal services MORE AVAILABLE to the middle and lower income people."*

Providing legal services to the masses at affordable rates not only provides an affordable service to individuals but also fulfills a necessary void in the all-powerful home-based business movement. With prices as low as $16 per month, home-based business entrepreneurs can put themselves in between the buyers and sellers of this product and turn chaos into a direct-selling cash machine.

A few of the most common and everyday areas where preventive legal services can prove helpful in one's personal and business life include:

- Unlimited telephone consultations for personal or business advice.
- Wills, premarital agreements or questions, estate planning.
- Home-based business questions, leases, contract signings, self-employment.
- Bankruptcy, partnership, forming a corporation.
- Guardianship, Social Security, health care issues.
- Nursing home arrangements, living will, name change.
- Real estate transactions, consumer problems, financial hardship, separations, divorce, lawsuit, discrimination.
- Auto transactions, creditor harassment, family disputes.
- Landlord/tenant problems, insurance questions, child spouse support.
- Escrow, debt collections, DUI/DWI.

With rates as low as $16 to $25 per month ($57 per month company rates) individual members receive unlimited toll-free attorney consultations; letters and phone calls on their behalf; document and contract review; will preparation; and moving traffic violations assistance. In summary, you will be able to sell the most cost-effective service providing advice for any personal or business legal matter, including bankruptcy, divorce, and even pre-existing situations.

Considering that in 1980 there were over 12 million lawsuits, in 1986 there were 81 million lawsuits, in 1991 there were 92 million lawsuits, and there were over 100 million lawsuits last year, it becomes crystal clear that selling affordable monthly membership for legal representation is a booming business. Memberships are designed for individuals and business owners who might not be able to afford the high price of legal representation (costing up to $250 per hour) that they would otherwise pay.

How much to get started:   Less than $500

Who to contact:   The Direct Selling Association, (202) 293-5760

**6. The Ultimate Tax Shelter—Prepaid Mortgages.** Prepaid mortgages have a potential market of approximately 52 million homeowners. On top of that, this business provides a service that will save people literally tens of thousands of dollars. We're talking over $70,000 on average!

- As a consultant, you can create a business advising others to prepay their mortgage either by making two payments per month instead of one, or by paying additional premium payments on a monthly basis along with their regular payment. The government has explained in various mortgage industry studies that $8 to $10 billion of mortgage problems exist because homeowners' mortgages are miscalculated. The error ratio has been put as high as 47.5 percent or nearly 1 out of 2 homeowners.

- Can you imagine offering any one of the 52 million homeowners who have a mortgage a way to literally save tens of thousands of dollars? On a typical mortgage that's an additional $50,000 to $100,000 as well as 10 more years of mortgage payments. Your new *customers will build equity in their homes 200 percent to 300 percent faster* and all for less than 10 percent of the average cost of refinancing!

- The prepaid mortgage business is easy to learn and only takes a few hours a week. You can start this business part time and after making a lot of money, do it full time. You can work either day or night and, if you desire, you can leverage your business by hiring others to duplicate your process and pay them commissions with no expense to you. Your business can offer homeowners a way to literally save a fortune on their mortgages, all without having to refinance; it's as easy as teaching people how to prepay their mortgages.

At least one company has even boiled down the presentation to an eight-minute video that explains the entire program to prospective customers. At the end of the video, the prospect can now make the decision to become a customer and fill out the one-page enrollment form and you collect the $395 fee. That's it!

You can be in the prepaid mortgage business for yourself, but not by yourself. Along with the prospect's eight-minute in-home client video

---

**HOW DOES THE PREPAID MORTGAGE BUSINESS MEASURE UP?**

- The business meets one of the vital needs of society . . . saving people money (on average $70,000).
- The business has huge market potential with nearly 52 million prospective clients.
- With the potential gross profit up to $300 per client in a program that is guaranteed to save people money, finding potential customers is not a difficult process.
- The business is easy to learn and takes only a few hours a week.
- You can work the business in the day or in the evening, whenever you have time.
- You can make money with other people's energy (OPE). In other words, you can bring on other representatives to work underneath you and receive an override on their sales.
- The business has a high profit margin for the business owner and a high perceived value to the customer.

---

presentation, companies provide specialized training and audio cassette tapes that walk you through every aspect of the mortgage consulting business, expensive 200-plus-page training manual, flip-chart presentation, word-for-word scripts, unique direct-mail systems, ads, telephone scripts, and background and product information. If you don't have a computer, no problem! The companies will prepare the analysis for you, same day, and most will do it free of charge! Companies even supply client brochures, door hangers, enrollment application supplies, and incredible software for under $500.

How much to get started:   Less than $500

Who to contact:   Randy Kusiak, AAA Financial Corporation, (800) 285-9114

## THE MSI GENERATION

You'll be able to start these businesses for as little as $50 to as much as $10,000, with most of them costing $500 or less. MSIs fit my profile for the ideal business because you can:

- Cut your commute from 40 minutes to 40 seconds.
- Mothball your suit and work in the comfort of your own home.
- Donate your high heels to charity.
- Be home for your children.
- Combine business and pleasure.
- Create instant cash flow.
- Reduce your taxes.
- Build your dreams, not someone else's.
- Free your creative mind, network, and compete.

MSI opportunists are people who want better jobs and are tired of rosy projections. Behind every rosy mathematical projection is the reality of the working-class American. The fact that the economy grew an average of 220,000 jobs per month in 1996 versus 180,000 in 1995 doesn't really have any impact on the average individual's ability to spend less than he makes. Does the fact that the mutual fund industry is expanding at $25 billion monthly or that companies are raising money in the stock market at a record pace mean you'll have more money to buy your children a new pair of $100 "Shaq Attack" basketball shoes? Or does the fact that the jobless rate in June 1996 dropped to its lowest rate of 5.5 percent and 348,000 new jobs were created allow the middle management or the working-class person to take a vacation in the style she truly deserves?

The answer is, No. Statistics such as those mentioned above will only have a direct effect on income months, or even years, down the line and only as long as they constantly improve. The fact is that these rosy projections clutter the reality that retail, temporary help, and health care jobs helped post the biggest gains in new jobs followed by construction. You and I both know that retail, temporary employment, and construction jobs are all fluctuating jobs that have the longevity of a hot air balloon with a slow leak. The reality is layoffs are more frequent, anxiety is higher, and net-of-inflation wages are rising a soft 0.6 percent a year ($^6/_{10}$ of a percent), half the pace of the 1980s. Eighty-six percent of large companies now outsource some services, compared with 58 percent in 1992. These numbers will drive the masses to MSI on an accelerated basis. These real-life statistics are reducing the average employee's request for wages and are driving millions to want better jobs. We want more job opportunities to lessen our dependence on factors beyond our control.

- The average person will work approximately 90,000 hours in his/her lifetime, while spending less than 10 hours planning his/her financial future. Although better than the norm, only 13 percent of state employees have taken advantage of savings bond payroll deduction programs.
- In Japan, the average worker has a lower salary than we do, higher inflation than we do, and he/she will save 17 percent of his/her pay annually. In Germany the same situation applies and the Germans save 11 percent of their salary. The average worker in America will save between 3 percent and 5 percent of his or her salary.
- 85 percent of men who reach the age of 65 do not even have $250 in the bank.[1]

Is it any wonder why the average individual is fed up with the instability and unmarketability of his training as he approaches the 21st century? Can it really be true that if you graduated from high school or obtained a college degree 5, 10, 15, 20, 25 years ago or more, then all that proves is that you were pretty smart a long time ago?

## MULTIPLE SOURCES OF INCOME (MSI) THROUGH THE 21st CENTURY

Gordon Moore, the co-founder of Intel Corporation, is quoted as saying, "You'll be able to talk into a computer and it will print out what you said. Or you will be able to type out a message in English—and it will be translated into Japanese, or Hindu, or Chinese instantly."[2]

The point is well made. Why would you ever need to go to a library or leave your home to research facts, figures, information, and ideas, when you can sit down in the comfort of your own home, turn on your communication devices, and have access to everything you need to know?

The experts predict that in 10 or 15 years, over half of the companies in existence will have telecommuting programs in place; 60,000 of the nations' 2 million federal workers nationwide will telecommute by the year 1998; 5,000 federal workers will have similar arrangements, spend-

---

1. Social Security Administration.
2. "Whither Moore's Law?" *Forbes,* September 11, 1995.

ing on average 1½ days a week at one of the 12 telecommuting sites open since 1990; and as many as 14 million telecommuters by the year 2000 will make up the most highly mobile, educated, and plugged-in workforce ever. Doesn't it make sense that this group will aspire to have more than one income-generating career at a time? By the year 2000, I believe that the average working American will perform an average of 2.5 projects at one time. What we're talking about is the definition of careers being redefined because the working class is highly motivated, connected, and able to satisfy its shorter attention span by leveraging its mind into multiple sources of income. Gone will be the days when employers have total control over employees and forbid their outside activities or tie them up so completely at work, on the factory floor, or in the office that carrying on other employment is only a dream.

Those who are computer literate will be able to talk into their computers by the year 2000, press a button, and, as Gordon Moore says, print out their dictation. You can only imagine the outlandish amount of possibilities and output that anyone of any background or economic profile with a little bit of training will be able to produce. The *computer illiterate* must answer this question:

> What is the product or service I can buy, sell, or represent to this mass movement of people moving toward home-based business and technology?

*Computer literates* will have a whole new set of possibilities, all having to do with making money with technology:

> How do I effectively manage the most effective communication tool in the history of humankind to distribute products and services to the masses for profit?

Open up your mind to the possibilities. Quietly sit back and plot your position as Generation Xers and Baby Boomers flee the corporate world in droves, crying out for the opportunity to take back control of their lives and leverage their minds to get paid what they're really worth.

## THE 40/50/40 PLAN

The 40/50/40 career plan—40 minutes commuting, working 50 hours a week for 40 years only to work harder and generate less money, time, and privacy—is an outdated system of corporate engineering. MSI will transfer any individual into the massive mainstream and provide the power to be self-sufficient and financially free. Watch closely as the speed of technology and the Telecommunications Act of 1996 kick off the start of the Information Age explosion. The masses will turn on their computers, watch less television, sleep less, read fewer books, and watch fewer soap operas. This will be the crossover point signaling massive financial opportunity. You'll know the time has come and the money will flow from every MSI opportunity you've selectively put in place between 1997 and the year 2001.

# Strategy #3: Reap the Rewards of Direct Selling

2 + 2 + 2 + 2 . . . Adds up to 8
2 × 2 × 2 × 2 . . . Will make you wealthy

Are you prepared for the future? Or have you prepared your life for an industry that has changed faster than you have? Our society has revolved around four major movements:

1. Engineering and manufacturing.
2. Information for decision making.
3. Technology for enhanced communication.
4. Distribution channels for effective marketing of products and services.

As a result of these movements, we've seen the economy grow from a labor-intensive workforce to one that is driven by management, communications enhanced by the speed of technology, and the use of mass distribution as the final conduit for providing goods and services into the marketplace.

Without a doubt, the next decade's money barons will be decided by who owns the distribution channels providing the gateway for any variety of products to be driven into the marketplace. This generates an enormous amount of revenue in a short period of time that's predictable based on past experience. For example: I was the group sales manager for the Carnation Company in 1981 and 1982. My responsibilities included the management of a team of approximately seven territory sales managers with all of us having responsibility for privately owned food service distribution companies. These companies had warehoused literally thousands of food service items of which the Carnation Company was one supplier. These distribution houses had their own fleet of trucks and sales people who would take orders from restaurants, school cafeterias, fast-food chains, and other related food service outlets, as well as deliver the products.

Each of our jobs was to get as many of our products stocked at each distributor we were responsible for and help that distributor sell as much product as possible by supporting their employees' education, sales training, and sales efforts. If my dollar volume at XYZ Distributor was $2 million annually of Carnation product and there were, say, 100 representatives like myself throughout the United States responsible for 500 distributors, you have a quick idea of the dollar volume created each time Carnation came out with a new product. Just imagine the impact of 100 representatives contacting 500 distributor organizations who control 3,000 of their own independent representatives calling on 100 customers. It's easy to understand the volume of sales each time Carnation introduced a new product to its distributors. How many times have you seen companies introduce new products on a regular basis and then reintroduce existing products as "New and Improved"? Just imagine what it does to the company's dollar volume of sales within the first 30 days when it introduces a new or existing product into the marketplace based on the exponential sales efforts already in place.

The person who controls the distribution system controls the flow of goods and services that affect your life. If you have a stockbroker or you own mutual funds, you'll notice that once you open up an account, the person who handles your account is the middleman and you become part of his or her distribution system. Whenever this person has new products, services, or recommendations, you'll notice he will continue to call you on a regular basis. Let's say a stockbroker has 300 clients and the broker comes up with one recommendation that generates an average $100 commission for each sale. Now let's assume 25 percent of the people purchase that specific recommendation. The broker has now generated 75 sales at an average $100 commission for total gross commissions of $7,500. Not a bad day's work.

How about your insurance representative? Once you purchase an insurance policy, whether it's a life insurance policy, disability insurance policy, or related coverage, you'll notice that once the initial sale is consummated, the agent always comes back and presents another related insurance product. For example, you purchased a life insurance product when you first decided to get life insurance coverage. You'll notice your agent always asks about your children or your spouse and always comes back for an annual review to make sure that you are never underinsured. Using an example similar to our stockbroker, say this insurance agent has 200 customers. The agent is in fact the middle person acting as an agent between the insurance company and the customer. If 15 percent of her customers increase their coverage annually, that's 45 additional sales without ever prospecting for a new customer. Now, let's say the agent gets 50 new customers during that same calendar year and an additional 15 percent of the existing database purchases a new policy. You can see the distribution system becomes an invaluable asset to the business and continually provides additional cash flow on a regular basis. The same power of being the middle person and controlling the distribution system holds true not only for the stockbroker or the insurance agent, but also the landscaper, the auto salesperson, the cleaning and laundry service, the Internet provider, the cable television provider, the digital satellite service provider, and so on. In this book, I've listed six of the hottest home-based business industries for the next five years. The fact is, once you understand the concept of middleman and distribution, you can literally go out there and find any product or service that you think is of exceptional value and for which you can create tremendous demand and literally approach those companies about brokering their product. Without ever taking inventory or paying anyone out of pocket, you can negotiate a relationship where you'll provide orders complete with credit cards and/or checks to these product companies who are willing to fill the order and pay you a commission. In 1996 alone, I've identified 16 specific products and/or opportunities and created marketing relationships with those companies with no out-of-pocket expenses for inventory. We currently market those products utilizing the incredible leverage of their name and product value to generate business—from which my wife and I receive income.

You can create a distribution system and use it for any product or service that you think adds tremendous value to the customer. Your customer, your contacts, people who have purchased your product in the past or who will purchase in the future—they all become part of your distribution system database. My wife and I came up with a product in 1995 that was a recruiting audiotape for a home-based business. Utilizing our database, we faxed our sales proposition, along with a special price for this product, to all of those customers and prospective customers on a regular basis. These potential customers received our solicitation over the fax machine complete with the order form and then could fax us back their orders with their credit card information for payment. For 10 consecutive months, we generated anywhere from $100 to $750 per day, seven days a week, on average, with the smallest order being for a minimum quantity of 25 tapes and the largest order being for 5,000 tapes. In this example, we had considered being the middle person for someone else's product, but when we realized how lucrative the product was and decided we could produce a more compelling product, we also became the product provider as well as the middleman.

Take advantage of the years of research I've conducted to uncover the six hottest industries in the entire home-based business market. These industries will truly put you on the path to profitability in the shortest time possible.

With the enhancements in computers, faxes, and modems, the key distinction is that you no longer have to be a major industry with hundreds of employees and tens of millions of dollars to compete for the same customers. Any person can crack the key to success by putting herself closer to the customer using some of the latest technology, which could be as simple as your phone and a fax machine, or as advanced as e-mail, web sites, and satellite television transmissions. The person who creates the partnership with the client will own the distribution channel by setting himself up as the middleman between the manufacturer and the customer.

Entrepreneurs command more respect because of their access to information and their ability to get close to the customer. The middleman almost always makes the most money for the least risk:

1. The highest paid businesspeople in the country are the middlemen: those who match buyers and sellers.

2. These supersuccessful entrepreneurs carry little or none of their own inventory. Instead, they always sell or broker someone else's product.

3. These megasuccesses spend minimum amounts for overhead expenses such as employees and large offices—their overhead sits on the top of their shoulders.

4. Top-selling entrepreneurs focus their businesses on unique products that have tremendous name recognition.

5. Business superstars find ways to get lead time on their competitors.

6. The most successful entrepreneurs develop or have access to a built-in channel of distribution for their products and services.

## COLLABORATIVE MARKETING

This is what I call "collaborative marketing": When a manufacturer chooses collaborative marketing as its distribution method, that means it does not put its product on expensive retail or wholesale shelves. Instead, the products are sold to consumers by middlemen, people who have obtained distributorship rights from the manufacturer or its affiliated distributor organizations. The traditional middlemen, such as the wholesaler and retailer, are replaced by the distributor, who deals directly with the manufacturer, the distributor organizations, and the consumer.

A distributor builds his or her business not just by selling products to consumers, but more importantly, by building a *direct distribution system* utilizing the latest technology or a direct-selling organization (network marketing) made up of other distributors also building their own businesses. The original distributor receives income not only from personal sales but also receives overrides from the other distributors in the business as well. Witness the explosion of network marketing companies that are either using or experimenting with this distribution concept: Gillette, Colgate–Palmolive, Coca-Cola, Avon, Tupperware, MCI, and Sprint. Two of the largest network marketing companies, Amway and Shaklee, both have over 1 million independent distributors and produce over $1 billion in sales annually. Theodore Lindauer, nationally recognized network marketing attorney, estimates that $15–$18 billion of business services were sold by five million active network marketers in 1995 alone; this is more than a $2 billion increase over the year before. Network marketers not only make a percentage override on individual sales, but they also receive overrides on other network marketers that they recruit into the business, as well as networkers that they recruit, and so on.

Today, prime opportunities exist with major companies selling their products through direct sales and network marketing. Some have even introduced direct-selling organizations, creating the most promising of the new distribution channels. *Direct selling* puts the manufacturer directly in touch with the consumer and meets all of the above criteria for entrepreneurial success. An IBM chairman, Lou Gerstner, said recently, *"If you are in an industry between the manufacturer and the customer . . . you are an endangered species."* The old distribution systems are changing and industries that previously bridged the gap between the manufacturer and the customer are being replaced.

Network marketing is even bigger in Japan than in the United States, with over $20 billion in annual sales.

To get an idea of the exceptional growth that's possible, imagine that Distributor A helps just one person a month start a business and that each distributor in the level immediately below does the same and that each distributor in the second level does the same and so on. Within a year, Distributor A will have built an organization of over 4,000 people![1]

## DISTRIBUTION

Let's go back to the 1920s to understand this era's belief in distribution:

**1.** Department stores. W. T. Grant was the first person to create a department store. His goal was to get closer to the customer. Instead of everybody driving around town making multiple stops at various spe-

---

1. Collaborative marketing or direct selling can be carried out in one of two ways:
   a. Using the latest technology you can go directly to potential consumers acting as the middleman without expensive overheads and making a markup on the cost of the product from the manufacturer or the distributor provider.
   b. Utilizing the new era of direct-selling organizations, you can benefit by building an organization of people who are also building their businesses for which you receive an override.

cialty stores, he created one central location called the department store. The problem was that government agencies regulated against stores larger than 20,000 square feet between the years 1920–1931. In 1931, the Free Trade Act was passed and department stores became a reality. No longer were legislatures opposed to department stores being a threat to the retail industry and the generally accepted ways of previously doing business.

**2.** Franchising. Franchising arose as the next form of distribution to get closer to the customer. This form of decentralized distribution was outlawed by the United States Congress in 1958. Franchising as an industry was finally approved by Congress in 1959 by approximately eight votes. Franchising is now a $758 billion industry and clearly has proven that the most effective means of distribution is to get closer to the customer.

**3.** Wal-Mart. Instead of being tied to the shopping centers, Wal-Mart came along with a new idea of distribution. Wal-Mart's concept was to get even closer to the consumer; in doing so, Wal-Mart leapfrogged Sears and became the world's largest retailer. Sales for 1996 were $45 billion, making the Wal-Mart family one of the richest families in the free world. Sam Walton's idea of putting his stores even closer to the customer in strip malls was the next evolution in the distribution cycle—further demonstrating the power of decentralized distribution.

**4.** Direct selling (network marketing). This system is leapfrogging over Wal-Mart today. It involves creating a partnership alliance with middlemen uniquely positioned between the manufacturer and the customer.

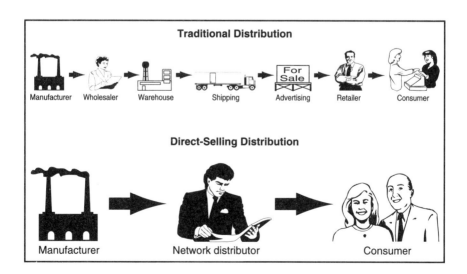

**Traditional Distribution**

Manufacturer   Wholesaler   Warehouse   Shipping   Advertising   Retailer   Consumer

**Direct-Selling Distribution**

Manufacturer          Network distributor          Consumer

This direct-selling system eliminates up to five levels of an awkward and outdated distribution system and puts the middlemen in a position to capture market share and revenue. This system allows an easy entry into the marketplace without outrageous marketing budgets and rewards the individuals who do the direct selling. To take this concept one step further, this new middleman provides greater education to potential customers with communication broadcasts and one-on-one selling, actual presentations and demonstrations, as well as personal order-taking. This evolutionary process will speed the delivery of products to market by anyone with access to a cost-effective distribution system, resulting in more commission dollars to the individual distributors and middlemen.

## INDEPENDENCE AND MEGAPROFITS: THE BENEFITS OF DIRECT SELLING

Every year, thousands of people discover the benefits of direct selling. Here are just a few:

**1.** Some of the most successful direct selling entrepreneurs are those who don't necessarily consider themselves to be top salespeople. Instead, they approach their business as an opportunity to educate or share with others, thus receiving significant rewards in addition to financial profit.

**2.** You're in business for yourself, but not by yourself. In other words, you take on relatively little personal risk. The company that makes the products or provides the services assumes all the cost of product research and development, manufacturing, quality control, training materials, and so on. The middleman is responsible for sales and building a distribution system.

**3.** As a direct salesperson, you get to set your own hours and determine your own working conditions. You can set up your virtual company in the comfort of your own home, doing the business part time or full time. You have total freedom.

**4.** In direct selling, the fastest road to success is to have people duplicate your success. That means assisting them in creating the same kind of organization, as well as teaching them to become top-notch coaches themselves. Direct selling utilizes the leverage that other people provide. If you perform only at your own maximum capability each day, that's all you'll ever get, but when your efforts are leveraged by others, the results are exponential ($2 + 2 + 2 + 2 + 2 + 2 + 2 + 2 + 2 + 2 = 20$, but when you multiply, $2 \times 2 \times 2 \times 2 \times 2 \times 2 \times 2 \times 2 \times 2 \times 2 = 1024$, a 51 times greater increase!).

**5.** In direct selling, you have the incomparable feeling of teamwork, leadership, and accomplishment that is so rare in today's corporate world. It's a highly charged, united sense of purpose that is rarely seen today outside of spectacular sporting events such as the Super Bowl.

# Strategy #4: Put Your Business on Autopilot by Investing in Technology

## VIRTUAL MONEY

Putting your business on autopilot to ensure the continued flow of residual income is as easy as commuting to your computer. We've already learned the secret that $2 + 2 + 2$ is simple mathematics but $2 \times 2 \times 2$ will make you wealthy. Your ability to perpetuate your income stream will allow you the freedom to enjoy your life with a no-nonsense approach to controlling information and communication.

The strategies listed in the accompanying box should be implemented early on in your MSI business. Your ability to control the business flow, expand new business, and retain your quality of life is tantamount to your success both personally and financially. There's nothing worse than going out and getting involved with a business only to have yourself, your spouse, or even your girlfriend or boyfriend hound you because you always seem to be running around like a chicken with its head cut off. Unless you start to take advantage of the business systems I'm about to explain, your business may never take off in the early years, and you may never be able to enjoy the freedom you've worked so hard to build.

## NINE STEPS TO RESIDUAL INCOME SUCCESS

**1.** Communication technology.

**2.** Caller ID organization.

**3.** Outbound e-mail blast and fax broadcasts.

**4.** Inbound e-mail and return communications.

**5.** Become a student of direct response marketing.

**6.** The remote control office.

**7.** New product distribution.

**8.** Internet selling made easy.

**9.** Cheap communication on the internet.

## VIRTUAL COMMUNICATIONS

Whenever you go out and build a distribution system having both customers and salespeople, you'll find that your time is completely eaten up by personal communications between those customers and salespeople from which you derive your income or overrides. It's critical that at this stage of your business you subscribe to a two-way voice communication system that allows you to communicate with everybody in your distribution selling network. One of the ways to manage a business that supplies products to customers is to keep every person in constant communication without having to return messages. The voice system should provide the following features:

- Humanlike, interactive voice interface.

- Global call announce anywhere.

- Virtual hallway: Ability to connect with colleagues regardless of location.

- Reminders: Automatic notification of important callbacks and action items.

- Voice-dialable online phone directory for up to 150 contacts and 750 numbers.

- Call routing to any location: priority calls or all calls.

- Message callback: Ability to return calls without hanging up or redialing.

- Labeled messages: Option to choose what to hear first and quickly sort messages by sender, time of arrival, and so on.

Such a system will multiply your chances for success and provide duplication to everyone throughout your distribution group. What this means to you in bottom-line dollars is greater profits from a more effectively communicating selling organization. You'll move more goods and services in a shorter period of time with the least amount of complication. One of the finest systems available is controlled by billionaire Craig McCaw. It's called the Magic Number system.[1]

## Inbound Communication

I recently ran across an inexpensive digital answering machine at Radio Shack's Incredible Universe Technology Warehouses called the Bogun Friday Communications Device.[2] Friday will give you seven voice boxes, each with a different message depending on which voice box the caller selects. Callers can select the appropriate box and hear a personalized message that will allow them to either place an order or explain specifically what their needs are. The product retails for approximately $170. This machine also will forward calls, bypassing the phone company so that you can respond at a moment's notice.

There also are products you can buy to enhance your computer system so that it acts as an answering machine complete with voice boxes, music on hold, follow-me features, as well as fax support. One such product is Delrina WinFax,[3] which allows you to fax directly from other software programs, automatically forwards faxes to another fax number, allows for remote retrieval of faxes, permits you to fax broadcasts to hundreds of people at a time, is compatible with database programs such as Symantec's Act! for Windows, and also allows sending and receiving of e-mail.

When it comes time to manage your database, you should consider programs such as Symantec's Act!™,[4] one of the top-rated and best-selling contact management systems available for the computer. The Act! software system will allow you to create a database and consolidate all of your meetings, contacts, follow-up letters, and the like in a single database that will also act as a daily planner. In short form, Act! will provide you with the ability to look at your daily calendar and see when you've

---

1. Magic Number, Darcy Hoffman (800)315-1876.
2. Bogun Communications, (800)942-6436.
3. Delrina WinFax, (800)441-7234.
4. Symantec's Act! Contact Management Software, (541) 465-8645.

scheduled an appointment to call a business associate, pull up the individual's profile while you're dialing the number, review your notes from past discussions, use the autodialer, and print out a follow-up letter with the stroke of a button.

## Communication Blast

Utilizing a simple distributor and customer database system, you'll want to include e-mail addresses and fax numbers as a standard business practice. With the 1997 introduction of personal communications devices for as little as $200–$300, you'll see the mass market move into the technology era. These personal communication devices, as well as portable and desktop computers, will allow every individual to communicate through very inexpensive e-mail and the Internet, versus paying the long distance charges for fax machines and phone calls. Personal communications devices that fit in your hand will rely on the computer and even the television as the screen. On a daily basis you will be able to go back and forth between e-mail and Magic Number systems, leaving up-to-date messages for literally thousands of distributors involved in your distribution system. You also will be able to access the latest updates for your travel schedule, seminar schedule, upcoming events, product news, deadlines, and money-making opportunities. Such flexibility is important because it lets everybody know that no matter where you are, you're on top of your business.

## Free Publicity

This program will work for anybody interested in creating marketing visibility and getting free publicity for their business, product, or service. At a cost of approximately 15¢ per fax, we fax a press release to radio stations based on the information from a program I do with Paul Hartunian, noted publicity expert, titled "How To Get $1 Million Worth of Publicity . . . Free!"[5] This simple one-page, third-grade-level, 300-word press release has turned out to be the cheapest way to generate tens of thousands of dollars in free publicity and sales of my products and services. And the amazing thing is, I stumbled on this method accidentally.

---

5. Paul Hartunian, "How To Get $1 Million Worth of Publicity . . . Free!" Fax requests to (619)259-8705.

I already faxed this press release to what I thought was a local radio station only to have it respond that it was in fact not a radio station, but that it represented 400 radio stations. It called me up within 15 minutes of the first discussion and did a mock interview over the phone to make sure I could talk about the subject in my press release related to home-based businesses. Completely satisfied, the station told me that it would promote my information to the 400 radio stations that it represents.

By utilizing press release strategies, literally anyone, from any walk of life, whether they are the local plumber, carpenter, or aspiring entrepreneur, can become a master marketer and promoter extraordinaire. The fax machine, e-mail, and other related communications tools that I've discussed allow you to manage and expand your business, utilizing vital communication systems. This process will minimize the amount of time you need to be involved and maximize the amount of free time for your personal enjoyment and pleasure.

## More on Inbound Communications

Keep in mind that your inbound communications on your E-mail or your fax machine continue to make your commute only as far as from your bedroom to your computer. You get up in the morning, put on your bathrobe, brush your teeth, walk around the corner, and collect all your messages. Perhaps your e-mail messages downloaded while you were sleeping through a variety of services such as the CompuServe Navigator add-on "Go Cissost"[6] or other related programs. Get yourself a cup of coffee, sit back, and leisurely review your faxes. Without ever picking up the phone, respond and fax back to those people who have contacted you. It's as easy as jotting down a few simple notes or comments and dialing up your fax machine. Ninety-nine percent of faxes require no more than a simple comment. e-mail is no different. As you sit back and review your e-mail over your computer, you can simultaneously e-mail back your responses and rest assured that your communication has been timely.

## THE ART OF THE STORY

Working out of your home from wherever you may be, I can guarantee you one of your most profitable endeavors to your business is the use of

---

6. CompuServe, (800)848-8990.

a direct-response marketing campaign. There are masters in this area, such as Dan Kennedy,[7] Jay Abraham,[8] Brad and Alan Antin,[9] and Rand Smith,[10] just to name a few. These are the people who write the compelling direct-marketing pieces that you and I receive in the mail and just can't seem to put down. You may be flipping through the newspaper and see a captivating ad with headlines that make you stop dead in your tracks and read on. These aren't the boring ads that you see on an everyday basis. Perhaps some of you have ventured to place an ad yourself only to find that your response rate is so depressing, you feel like it was a total waste of your money. These people are masters in the art of creating ads and other marketing materials that evoke emotional responses; they use right-brain thinking to write ads and direct-marketing pieces that really get people to act. These experts can predict, based on the number of ads and direct mail pieces they send, how many people will pick up the phone and call to order your product.

A good friend of mine, Rand Smith, a highly recognized real estate agent in Monterey, California, demonstrated to me just how powerful this marketing system can truly be for the aspiring entrepreneur. Rand started out in the real estate business with something less than a bang. Dismal is really the word he would use to describe his performance. Closing five, six, or sometimes seven transactions a year for more than a decade, he just kept grinding out his average little numbers.

Rand's office used all of the latest buzzwords and Rand went to all of the latest seminars, but still he could not seem to increase his numbers and get himself out of the broke, bored, and defeated state of mind he had put himself in.

Wearing cheap suits, avoiding simple technology such as voice mail, computers, and cellular phones, Rand continued to buy gas $10 at a time while paying the minimum every month on maxed-out credit cards.

Rand made a decision at that point in his life and in less than 30 months' time, Rand went from doing an average of six–seven transactions a year to listing and selling over 500 properties—likely one of the most dramatic turnarounds in real estate history. He went from being a survivor-oriented, never-invest-in-yourself, hope-for-the-phone-to-ring kind

---

7. Dan Kennedy, (602)997-7707.
8. Jay Abraham, (310)265-1840.
9. Antin Marketing Group, (800)848-9031.
10. Rand Smith, Seminars International, (800)404-7263.

of guy, to hiring four full-time assistants just to field the 120-plus incoming phone calls he generated each and every day.

Here's an even more remarkable piece of the story . . . Rand did all of this without prospecting. That's right. No cold-calling people at all hours of the day or night or bothering his friends by selling them products and services they didn't need. Studying some of the masters of direct marketing, people like Jay Abraham, Dan Kennedy, and Brad and Alan Antin, Rand developed his own "emotional response marketing system" that he operates on a day-to-day basis from the comfort of his own home and office, producing incredible results.

## INTERNET SELLING MADE EASY

You are sitting in a seminar audience and the lecturer asks, "How much is your advertising budget?" He's talking fast now and he rattles off a succession of additional questions all related to marketing and the success of your business. How much time have you spent developing a catchy headline for your ad? What markets are you targeting? What income brackets are most attracted to your product? And finally, the question that really hits home for your small business, "What percentage of monthly sales are you allocating to your advertising budget?"

It doesn't take too long for you to slink slowly down in your chair and get a little depressed because no one schooled you in the fine art of advertising and the simple fact is, you have no advertising budget. It's not that you don't believe in advertising, but the fact is that by age 17, the average child has watched 25,000 advertisements. You see Ronald McDonald, the Budweiser Clydesdales, and the Marlboro Man so many times that you can recite the Winston cigarette jingle from 20 years ago ("Winston tastes good like a cigarette should"), and if you see Nike's "Just Do It" slogan one more time you'll scream. The Jack in the Box clown has come back from being blown up more times than you've been to Jack in the Box, and if you get one more pitch in the mail touting, "Make $500 per day walking to your mailbox," you just might fill it out and send it back.

Well, your time has come. Forget the fact that you don't have an advertising or marketing degree or an Ivy League education. The Internet levels the playing field and allows every individual to create a Madison Avenue advertisement for pennies on the dollar. It can work for anyone who has basic typing skills, can read boiler plate text, or has a friend who will offer to sit down at a computer and type in your company profile. Now, computer illiterates and geniuses alike can create a Madison Avenue marketing program in the comfort of their own home promoting their own small business. The success stories range from small airlines offering discounted seats creating 100 percent profits on last-minute availability to mom-and-pop operations selling $5 pamphlets and books and even non-profit organizations doubling and tripling charitable donations.

Online success stories are sprouting up everywhere and you can participate in this marketing bonanza.

Recently I sat down with the recognized Internet marketing experts at Internet Interface Systems, Inc., in San Jose, California. Their clients range from manufacturers, retailers, and real estate companies to network marketing companies and seminar leaders. We discussed how to make money on the Internet. By using these steps, you can join thousands of small businesses that are using the Internet to build profits without spending a lot of time or money. These steps will increase your profits and put you on the road to mailbox money without the mailbox hype.

The Internet and the World Wide Web (the Web) are the next mass media and a powerful new marketing tool where your business can easily profit. Below are a few compelling reasons to establish your presence on the Web.

- Reach over 30 million "new" customers (and growing).
- Expand your geographic reach—go worldwide overnight.
- Get immediate customer feedback.
- More powerful than the Yellow Pages (at a fraction of the cost).
- Your Web site works for you all day . . . everyday—you're always open for business.
- Cheaper than print, radio, or TV.
- Receive and confirm orders.
- Post your basic business information . . . address, phone numbers, hours of operation.
- Heighten interest in your company.
- Release time-sensitive materials.
- Serve and educate your customers.
- Publish answers to frequently asked questions (FAQ).
- Stay in contact with your salespeople.

- Open the door to international markets.
- Test market new services and products.
- Reach the media.
- Generate leads.
- Gain a competitive edge.

Your Web site launches your high-tech marketing campaign and may include the following:

- Your company logo.
- A letter from your president.
- Product listing and information.
- Product order form.
- Electronic mail (e-mail) link.
- Customer surveys.
- Contest promotion.
- Contact information.
- Product information.
- Product specifications and drawings.
- Photos of your products.
- Photos of your company location/headquarters.
- Newsletter.
- Customer feedback.

I recently convinced the Web site experts at IIS who custom tailor Web sites that cost as much as $1500 to do a special promotion for *Wealth Starts at Home* readers.

Now you've created an international billboard marketing program in the comfort of your own home, to be delivered via your Web site. List your Web site with all the major search engines. Send out postcards and announce your Web site to both existing and potential customers and after every form of communication (i.e., business card, letterhead, etc.), list your Web site address. These simple steps will produce great results from many online marketers and put you on the fast track to level the marketing playing field with companies 10, 20, 30, or even 100 times your size.

Remember, if you don't get in the game, you'll never hit a home run.

## UP TO $1,500 FREE WEB SITE

The management at Internet Interface Systems, Inc. (IIS) have agreed to develop a free Web site for all *Wealth Starts at Home* readers. Not only will you receive a free 3-page Web site—a home page, a product page, and an order page—you'll be able to make online changes to your Web site as often as you wish. You don't even need to own a computer to open yourself up to over 30 million people who have Web access—without making a capital investment or spending money on staff time. You sell your prospects 24 hours a day, even when your business is closed, as well as being placed strategically in David D'Arcangelo's worldwide business network that will assure you traffic on a day-to-day basis. If you'd like to preview the site call 1-800-510-1020.

Call 1-800-510-1020 today toll-free to order your Free Web Site Kit up to a $1,500 value. Just fill out the simple instructions, mail it back to IIS, and your Web site is up and running. The only cost to you is the monthly hosting fee that all Web site owners pay to maintain their site on the Web. When calling 1-800-510-1020 make sure you mention that you are a David D'Arcangelo's *Wealth Starts at Home* reader.

## THE REMOTE CONTROL OFFICE

No one ever sits still for too long, especially when business is good and checks continue to roll in. Travel the country and the world, spend time with your children and grandchildren, sail your boat, walk the beach, give back to your church and your community, control your distribution system through a laptop computer that will allow you to connect to your computer from anywhere in the world.[11] These are just a few of the advantages to marketing your business through technology.

---

11. Server Technologies—Power On/Off, approximately $170, 1-800-835-1515.

# Strategy #5: Create a Tax-Free Windfall

The definition of insanity is to keep doing what you've been doing and expect things to change.

## THE CHALLENGE

The tips I'm about to share with you can help you turn your home business into the outrageously successful money machine that you have always wanted. As you saw from the story of my friend Jerry, starting a home business allows you to translate your major expenses into major tax deductions. Gone is the thinking that turns $1 of gross income into 50¢ of take-home pay. Net out your expenses and you're left with 3¢–5¢ to invest in a hopeless game plan for your financial future. Make an additional dollar profit and you'll pay additional taxes that drive down the value of that dollar to 50¢–75¢.

If you think your lifeline is Social Security and that if all else fails you'll be able to exist on the government's subsidy from your paid Social Security taxes, think again. The unemployment liabilities of private pension plans topped $50 billion in 1993 and federal officials screamed to the high heavens. This unfunded liability amounts to a mind-boggling $12 trillion. The public and congressional leaders now are pursuing reforms that would cost the system $1 billion per year; they want to triple the amount today's working seniors can earn before losing benefits, with other benefit cuts ready to pay for it. The ratio of workers to retirees is falling from 159 to 1 in 1940 to 3.3 to 1 in 1995, and that number will hit 2 to 1 in the year 2030.[1]

In other words, if we keep doing what we've been doing, we can expect less and less income from other sources to support us, which is what many retirees now depend on. The truth is staring us in the face, "Nobody cares more about you than you." If the average American is living off of $12,000 per year, a large percent of which is Social Security, and Social Security is dwindling, then it's obvious that in the future Social Security taxes will go up and a larger chunk of money will be taken out of your monthly check. The government will extend the current retirement age of 65 and make workers continue to work additional years before they can take their Social Security retirement income in order to make up for the dwindling funds. The statistics point to the fact that you'll be paying in more and waiting longer to get your money because the system is underfunded and there are less workers paying for each person retiring.

Pay particular attention to the accompanying table taken from *USA*

## Your Money's Worth?

| Year of Retirement | Age in 1996 | Current Law | With Tax Increases[a] |
|:---:|:---:|:---:|:---:|
| 1982 | 79 | 16.58 | N/A |
| 1987 | 74 | 6.98 | N/A |
| 1992 | 69 | 4.22 | N/A |
| 1997 | 64 | 1.42 | N/A |
| 2002 | 59 | −0.36 | N/A |
| 2007 | 54 | −1.41 | N/A |
| 2012 | 49 | −1.76 | N/A |
| 2017 | 45 | −1.56 | −1.58 |
| 2022 | 40 | −1.52 | −1.66 |
| 2027 | 35 | −1.72 | −2.07 |
| 2032 | 30 | −1.18 | −1.87 |
| 2037 | 25 | −0.70 | −1.81 |
| 2042 | 20 | −0.34 | −1.86 |
| 2047 | 15 | −0.13 | −2.04 |
| 2052 | 10 | −0.02 | −2.29 |
| 2057 | 5 | 0.08 | −2.54 |
| 2062 | 1 | 0.18 | −2.80 |

Note: [a] Payroll tax increases projected to keep Social Security solvent. Source: Tax Foundation.

Source: *USA Today*, March 19, 1996.

---

1. *USA Today*, March 19, 1996.

*Today,* (March 19, 1996) and decide if your money invested in Social Security will take care of you in the lifestyle you truly deserve. A 40-year-old person in 1996 will get an average annual rate of return on his investment dollars paid into Social Security of –1.52 percent. Now, keep in mind, if you put your money into a savings account or a money market account, you'd get approximately 4–5 percent per year, U.S. long-term Treasury bonds would pay 7 percent, and if you invested your money in blue chip stocks over the last 20 years you would have averaged approximately 14 percent per year.

## THE SECRETS OF INVESTING FINALLY REVEALED

In our discussion of Stratety #1, not only did we get a better understanding of the effective tax benefits of starting a home-based business, but we also learned about the incredible opportunity we have to put away tax-deferred and tax-free money. We learned that we can put members of our family into our business and utilize income shifting strategies to increase our before-tax income while at the same time, tax deferring up to 15 percent of our income as the major wage earner.

Let's take this whole process one step further and understand that Jerry and Linda in our money machine strategy are an average age of 40 years old. Their goal is to be financially free by age 60, having done absolutely no planning prior to age 40. Between the ages of 20 and 40 years old, Jerry and Linda went along from week to week, month to month, and year to year, living from check to check, having never saved a dime. In the example you will see below, Jerry wants to save $10,000 per year tax

The $1 Million Tax Subsidized Family Fortune in 20 Years

| Jerry's SEP–IRA: $10,000 per year; Value in 20 years | Linda's SEP–IRA: $2,000 per year; Value in 20 years | John, age 8: $2,000 per year tax free; Value in 20 years | Mary, age 10: $2,000 per year tax free; Value in 20 years |
|---|---|---|---|
| ⬇ | ⬇ | ⬇ | ⬇ |
| $630,000 tax deferred | $126,000 tax deferred | $126,000 | $126,000 |
| **Total family fortune totally tax deferred and tax free = $1,008,000** | | | |

deferred into a SEP–IRA account and Linda plans to put $2,000 a year into her SEP–IRA account and income shift $2,000 to each child every year totally tax free, utilizing the IRS standard deduction.

## THE POWER OF TAX DEFERRAL

Not only have Jerry and Linda been building a $1 million family fortune, they also have taken advantage of the IRS tax benefits to put money back in their pockets. In other words, using the money machine concept and the work efforts of Jerry, Linda, and their children, the IRS has subsidized their family with tax-deferred and tax-free money benefits that will allow them to create a $1 million family fortune. If you think this money machine concept is trivial, let me take you one step further with the following illustration. Let's compare $30,000 invested one time taxable at the rate of 33 percent annually (see Table A) over 10-, 20-, 30-, and 40-year periods of time at various investment rates of return. Now compare this with the money machine strategies investing $30,000 on a totally tax-deferred basis (see Table B) utilizing the same variables. Pay attention to how the money machine strategies will impact the quality of your lifestyle and the future at no extra expense.

Table A: $30,000 Gross Investment
(33% Average Tax Rate)

| Years | Return 8% | Return 10% | Return 12% |
|-------|-----------|------------|------------|
| 10 | $ 50,568 | $ 57,381 | $ 65,008 |
| 20 | $ 85,239 | $109,751 | $141,868 |
| 30 | $143,679 | $209,920 | $305,252 |
| 40 | $242,188 | $401,512 | $661,461 |

Now let's look at the same $30,000 utilizing the money machine strategy to invest it on a tax-deferred basis over the same period of time:

Table B: $30,000 Gross Investment
(Tax Deferred)

| Years | Return 8% | Return 10% | Return 12% |
|-------|-----------|------------|------------|
| 10 | $ 64,768 | $ 77,812 | $ 93,875 |
| 20 | $139,829 | $ 201,825 | $ 289,389 |
| 30 | $301,880 | $ 523,482 | $ 898,798 |
| 40 | $651,786 | $1,357,778 | $2,791,549 |

Now, let's compare these two scenarios of $30,000 taxable and $30,000 tax deferred and see what the result is after 40 years if you have to live off your investment at 10 percent a year.

| Amount | $30,000 Taxable | $30,000 Tax Deferred |
|---|---|---|
| Value, year 40 | $1,357,778 | $401,512 |
| Annual income at 10% | $ 401,512 | $ 40,100 |

The benefit of the money machine strategy is obvious as it provides an approximate three-to-one return (300 percent) versus having your money taxed on an annual basis. We can see that, while we start with the same $30,000 for each strategy, when utilizing the home-based business

## TWO IS 100 PERCENT BETTER THAN ONE

One of the greatest benefits of having a home business is that you can also open up a SEP–IRA, even if you already participate in a retirement plan with your current employer. Even if you work two jobs, the only way the IRS will allow you to have two retirement plans is if your second plan is part of your own home-based business. Why is it important to double the benefit by creating another tax deferred plan with your SEP–IRA?

| How Taxes Add Up | Taxpayer |
|---|---|
| 31 % | Federal tax |
| 4 % | State tax |
| 15.3% | Self-employment tax |
| 10 % | "Sin taxes" |
| 65 % | |

You may think you're in a lower tax bracket, but when you add up the federal taxes, state taxes, self employment taxes, and "sin taxes," you can see how much of your money goes to the government. Sin taxes are the taxes that the federal and state governments place on products that you and I consume on a regular basis, such as automobile sales taxes, gasoline taxes, property taxes, airline ticket taxes, hotel taxes, taxes on clothing, and so on. If you make $20/hour, it takes two hours' work ($40) to get one hour ($20) of net take-home pay. When utilizing after-tax dollars, we reduce our buying power even more with sin taxes, thereby purchasing even less with our money. By utilizing tax-deferral and tax-free strategies, we can immediately give ourselves up to a 100 percent raise.

money machine program, you can live three times the lifestyle you'd be able to live on taxable money. Let's keep in mind that we're not even taking into consideration any other benefits to your home-based business program.

## THE LIFESTYLE QUESTION

My next question is, if you get three times the return on the same amount of dollars using the money machine tax-deferred concept, then, "How many more years would you have to work, if you continued to pay taxes annually on your money, to equal the amount of money you could make using the money machine tax-deferred concept?" The answer is obvious: You would have to work three times as long. Or your money would have to work three times harder. In other words, you could come up with three times the amount of money or let your money work three times as long to take home the same amount of money that we created on a tax-deferred basis using the money machine concept.

If you want to accelerate your program using these concepts, all you need to do is add additional money to maximize your SEP–IRA benefits. You'll notice that in Jerry and Linda's case, they could put in 15 percent of their salary under the SEP–IRA guidelines up to a maximum of $22,500. Jerry was only putting in $10,000 and based on Linda's salary she was able to contribute $2,000. If you want to start with smaller amounts of money, the effects are just as dramatic and, with the power of compounding, it's never too late to get started.

### The Turtle versus the Rabbit

Just imagine, if I were to approach you (and let's assume you're a mediocre golfer, like myself) and I asked you if you'd like to play a round of golf for $10,000 per hole . . . Your response would probably be a very strong "No!" Then, what if I said, "Well, since we're friends, let's go out and play 18 holes and bet a very conservative 10¢ a hole, just for fun." You'd probably say, "Okay." And then what if I turned around and said, "Since we're just playing for fun, let's play a harmless 10¢ a hole and double it each hole."

You'd probably still go along with me and say "Okay." Ten cents a hole, doubled for 18 holes in a golf match equals $13,107.20 after 18 holes.

As you can see, it's never too late to get started and, in today's marketplace, mutual fund companies will accept amounts of as low as $1 to

It's Never Too Late

At the first hole, it's 10¢.
At the second hole, it's 20¢.
At the third hole, it's 40¢.
At the fourth hole, it's 80¢.
At the fifth hole, it's $1.60.
At the sixth hole, it's $3.20.
At the seventh hole, it's $6.40.
At the eighth hole, it's $12.80.
At the ninth hole, it's $25.60.
At the tenth hole, it's $51.20.
At the eleventh hole, it's $102.40.
At the twelfth hole, it's $204.80.
At the thirteenth hole, it's $409.60.
At the fourteenth hole, it's $819.20.
At the fifteenth hole, it's $1,638.40.
At the sixteenth hole, it's $3,276.80.
At the seventeenth hole, it's $6,553.60.
At the eighteenth hole, it's $13,107.20.

open an account. Shop around and you'll find that there are even a few mutual fund companies such as John Hancock, MSF, Pioneer, American Capital, and Vanguard Funds that will allow you to open custodian accounts and act as the custodian for your children or grandchildren.

## THE $7,500 BUSINESS SUCCESS BONUS

Keep in mind the simplified employee pension (SEP) is the easiest place for small business owners to start their retirement plan. Your written plan allows you to make contributions for your own, as well as your employees', retirement without getting involved in the more complex plans. Most financial institutions will be happy to help you put this program in place at little or no cost.

An added benefit is that the SEP plan can also include a salary reduction program, which means employees could have part of their pay deducted and contributed to their SEP–IRA. This money is also tax deferred.

The bonus program begins when you've maxed out your SEP–IRA plan. You're putting in 15 percent of your salary, up to $22,500, and you'd like to continue to tax defer more money because your business is really beginning to boom. In Jerry and Linda's case, the next step was to open a KEOGH plan. There are two basic kinds of KEOGH plans: defined benefit plans and defined-contribution plans. You may have two KEOGH plans, but the contribution to all the plans may not exceed the overall limit. In other words, whereas you have a retirement plan at your full-time job and you open a SEP–IRA with your home business, you can max out contributions to whatever the limits are for both plans. The KEOGH plan works best in the home-based business if you either have no other plan at your full-time job or have decided to make your home-based business your full-time career. At that point you can maximize the KEOGH plan in either the defined-benefit plan or the defined-contribution plan and raise your limit from 15 percent of your salary up to $22,500 to 25 percent of your salary up to $30,000 per year. **That's a $7,500 tax-deferred bonus!** The benefits of home-based business are generally exhausted when there are no other employees, or at the most one, and you maximize benefits for yourself and your employee/spouse and/or children. Most mutual fund companies, discount brokerage firms, or your broker can help you set up and decide which one of the plans will best suit your needs and maximize your deductions.

## LIFESTYLE IS A CHOICE

If the prospects of retiring and getting a negative return on the money you've paid in to Social Security irritate you, it should be crystal clear that no one cares more about your retirement than you. The bottom line is you have one investment that's guaranteed to lose money and that's Social Security. Every month and every year that you continue to pay money in, you are assured of the fact that your return on your money won't even keep up with the rate of inflation. The alternatives are now better than ever . . . the timing is perfect to position yourself in the way of the home-based business movement . . . the six hottest industries for home-based business will give you the greatest chance of success . . . the middleman always makes the most money and controls distribution . . . the IRS will literally subsidize your business with tax benefits . . . by making the decision to take back control of your life and go home on a part-time basis, you'll be able to create three times the lifestyle than working for someone else. It doesn't cost any extra money to utilize these strategies. The strategies don't discriminate against anyone who is willing to make the effort. When would be the best time to start?

# Strategy #6: Turn Your Major Expenses into a Profit Center or Tax Deduction

Turn every major expense into a profit center, build equity, and generate income.

Now that you understand the rules of the game of money, you can utilize the Bucket Story (see Strategy #7) as your own personal game plan to achieve your goals and objectives. Whether you have a home-based business or not, the strategies I'm about to describe will work in almost every situation. They will allow you to maximize every dollar of income.

Following are a few tips on how to fill up Security Bucket #1 quicker.

- Cut credit card interest up to 100 percent.
- Build your cash reserves up to 100 percent faster.
- Take advantage of life insurance loopholes.
- Utilize IRA, SEP, 401(k), and retirement plans.
- Investigate the $100,000 education funding solution.

## CREDIT CARDS FOR BUSINESS OR PLEASURE

Simplify your life and obtain two credit cards, one for business and one for pleasure. Immediately shift and transfer any balances you have on credit cards with rates in excess of 15 percent to cards with rates of 9 percent or 10 percent. This process will do two things for you: (1) it will immediately lower your 15–18 percent credit card rates to 9–12 percent, thereby providing you with an up-to-50-percent discount on the interest you're paying; and (2) you'll simplify your recordkeeping for your home-based business and your personal expenditures.

This strategy may be oversimplified, but it will help you begin to accumulate more money in your Security Bucket. In 1980 certificate of deposit (CD) rates peaked at 18 percent and have since fallen to 5 percent to 7 percent—yet most credit card rates have moved from 18 percent to 15 percent. It's not difficult to figure out who keeps the spread between 5 percent CD rates and 15 percent credit card rates.

Use the companies in the accompanying table or any of the major financial magazines to get an update of the cheapest rates for the consumer credit card. Look carefully at cards that benefit your particular situation, depending on whether you pay off your loan each month or carry a balance. Request checks for balance transfer. Ask them if once you receive your checks you can write out one of these checks on the new credit card to pay off the entire balance of the old credit card and reduce your interest up to 100 percent. I call this debt shifting.

### The Best Credit-Card Deals in the United States

Carry a Balance

| Card | Rate | Fee | Telephone |
|------|------|-----|-----------|
| Pulaski B&T (Ark.) | 9.45% | $35 | 800-980-2265 |
| Wachovia Bank (Del.) | 8.25% | $88 | 800-842-3262 |
| Metropol. Natl. (Ark.) | 9.96% | $25 | 800-883-2511 |
| Federal Savings (Ark.) | 9.35% | $33 | 800-374-5600 |

Pay in Full

| Card | Rate | Fee | Telephone |
|------|------|-----|-----------|
| AFBA Industrial (Colo.) | 11.40% | $0 | 800-776-2265 |
| Horizon B&T (Texas) | 12.90% | $0 | 800-571-3462 |
| USAA Fed. Svgs (Texas) | 12.50% | $0 | 800-922-9092 |
| Metro. Svgs/Cleveland | 13.90% | $0 | 800-837-6058 |

## INCREASE YIELDS AND CASH RESERVES UP TO 100 PERCENT

Along with your two credit cards for your business and personal use, you need to open two money market accounts and close any of your checking accounts. If you currently have money in your checking account, it's obvious that you're in a money losing situation. You and I should be in the business of banking once we fully understand how checking accounts work. We put our money in the bank and it pays us *no interest, charges us fees,* and charges more than necessary for additional checks. On the other hand, we all know that the bank turns around and invests that money and charges 7–10 percent for home loans, 12–13 percent for personal loans, and 15–18 percent for a credit card. Who wrote the rules to this game?

Pay close attention when you run up a balance on your credit card. If you want to get out of debt, always pay more than the minimum payments, as you can see in the example below. A $2,000 balance with an annual interest rate of 19 percent and a minimum payment of $40 per month will take eight years and $3,904 to pay off completely. In our example, see how an extra $10 a month shortens your debt cycle to five years and $2,543—a savings of three years and $1,361.

Money Market Fund Bank Account

|  | Smart Money | Foolish Money |
| --- | --- | --- |
| Credit card balance | $2,000 | $2,000 |
| Payment | $40.00 (2% min. payment) | $50.00 (add an extra $10.00) |
| Years to pay off | 8 | 5 |
| Total paid | $3,904 | $2,543 |

## High Rates and Safe Money

Open two money market accounts at a brokerage firm or a mutual fund company and it will pay you interest on your money. Most will also allow you to write checks on an unlimited basis. In other words, you give them the money, they pay you interest at the current money market rates, and your money sits. If you want additional checks, just ask and most companies will send you personalized checks free!

Sample: Twelve Top Money Market Funds

| Taxable | | Tax-Exempt | |
|---|---|---|---|
| 1. Fidelity Spartan | 800-554-3902 | 1. Strong | 800-368-3863 |
| 2. Strong Heritage | 800-368-3863 | 2. Vanguard Muni | 800-662-7447 |
| 3. Alger[a] | 800-992-3863 | 3. Evergreen | 800-235-0064 |
| 4. Vanguard Prime | 800-662-7447 | 4. Calvert | 800-368-2748 |
| 5. Old Premium Plus | 800-872-6533 | 5. Kemper | 800-231-5142 |
| 6. Dean Whitter Active Assets | 800-367-7732 | 6. Putnam[b] | 800-225-1581 |

[a] Minimum deposit $1.

[b] Minimum deposit $500.

## Increase Yields Up to 100 Percent

Make your cash reserve in both your business or your personal account work harder and create more income. The simple guideline for this strategy is that you must subject your longer-term money to a little more volatility to achieve greater rates of return. This concept is very straightforward: "I find an investment that will pay me an above-average rate of return while I'm waiting for something to happen." This "safe money" could create an additional profit on your investment. The additional profits I'm speaking of are from some of America's leading multibillion dollar companies that currently are undervalued or out of favor. Out-of-favor stocks generally trade at a discount to real value. Take the money you're not in need of over the next 12–36 months and subject it to a little more volatility. Shift your money from the money market account into a stock account and purchase some of America's largest and most stable companies that pay competitive dividends. With a little research, you can find companies that are out of favor, meaning that the stock price is undervalued.

One example is a company we've all grown up with: Texaco. Texaco is undervalued based on its market value. After getting stock in the $60-per-share range paying a 5 percent dividend, the stock has run up as high as 88¾ in the last 52 weeks. As of July 1, 1996, the stock settled at $83.875 with the yield down to 3.8 percent. That's a 33 percent unrealized capital gain plus your original 5 percent yield—for a total return of 38 percent over the last 12 months (52 weeks). You're currently making 5.5 percent on your 1-year certificate of deposit, where your money is tied up for one year under penalty of early withdrawal. In our example, in purchasing Texaco stock at $60 per share paying a 5 percent dividend, we bet that Texaco would, at the worst, stay at the same price but hopefully move up in price before there was a need for the cash. When you own stock, you also are subject to the downside, so you should be prepared to hold your stock through the downs until the market recovers.

I've compiled a list of companies that provide above-average dividends while at the same time providing an opportunity for upside appreciation. This is timely information, and it's for sample purposes only. As time moves on, you should seek out additional companies trading below market value with upside appreciation.

### Dividend-Paying Stock with Upside Potential

| Company | Yield (8/96) |
| --- | --- |
| AT&T | 2.4% |
| Chevron | 3.7% |
| Exxon | 3.8% |
| JP Morgan | 3.64% |
| DuPont | 2.74% |
| Philip Morris | 3.77% |
| 3M | 3.04% |
| GM | 3.2% |
| Texaco | 3.9% |

## WHY LIFE INSURANCE?

Life insurance is without a doubt one of the most misunderstood products in the United States today. The fact is, you have short-term insurance needs that you'll cover with term insurance and long-term insurance needs for which you'll utilize "permanent" insurance policies. These policies could be either permanent policies purchased in your business or policies for individual members of your family. In this chapter, you'll find a list of contacts to call for insurance quotes so you'll know exactly how much and what type of policy to purchase. Most people should seek out a licensed insurance agent to properly plan their business and personal insurance needs. Learn to maximize the value of your policies in order to provide the maximum death benefit to your heirs and use cash value buildup within permanent policies to your benefit.

Review the insurance cost comparison of the various types of policies for a 40-year-old male in good health looking for a $500,000 death benefit policy. Pay particular attention to Strategy #7, which will go into detail regarding how to maximize the tax benefits included with various life insurance company–related products.

Baseball players strive to hit a .333 average, basketball players shoot 40 percent from 3-point range, and movie studios would be world champions if 50 percent of their movies were blockbusters, but the odds are the highest, 100 percent, that we'll all die someday. *If you have a 100 percent chance of dying, then why do it for free?*

Let's look at our basic needs and rank our priorities from most important (1) to least important (7):

| | |
|---|---|
| Home insurance | 5 |
| Health insurance | 3 |
| Auto insurance | 6 |
| Retirement plan | 4 |
| Steady income | 2 |
| Disability insurance | 7 |
| Your own life | 1 |

This may seem like a simple task, but what it does is make you prioritize and put a value on seven areas of your life. Take a look back and reflect on how you prioritized the most valuable assets in your life and ask yourself, "Have I ensured the priorities in my life?" It's interesting to find out and compare your priorities. Generally, 100 percent of people have their home insured, 75 percent of people have their auto insured, 75 percent have their life insured, and only 25 percent have their income insured.

If you don't insure the machine that creates the money (you), and you're incapable of producing income, for whatever reason, then there will be no need to own home and auto insurance, and so on. The fact is, there is a 1 in 1,160[1] chance of a fire breaking out in your home, a 1 in 250 chance of something happening to your automobile, and a 27 out of 100 chance of dying at age 40—yet there is a 48 out of 100 chance of some type of disability, in excess of 90 days, for a 40 year old.

## Rules for Buying Life Insurance

If You're Going to Die, Why Do It for Free . . . ?

When I was a child growing up, it always seemed that life insurance salespeople found my dad too irresistible. There we were, a hard-working, middle-class family with four boys all under five years old and no life insurance. Not only did we not own a life insurance plan, but my dad had

---

1. Accidents Facts, National Safety Council, 1975 edition, National Center for Health Statistics, 1973 Society of Actuaries, 1973 Presentations Reports.

no retirement plan, which meant that the day he retired at age 65, his retirement balance was zero. It seemed on a monthly basis the insurance
agent would continue to make calls on our home, schooling my dad on
the hardships it would cause if anything happened to him. As the story
went month after month, "the family would never stand a chance and the
kids would probably never amount to much because of the lack of funds
for a college education."

Well, that's probably the last thing you ever want to say to an im-
migrant second-generation Italian. My dad was a proud man who worked
his entire life to teach values and morals, and put a roof over his family's
head. He tried to give our family everything we needed so we could assume responsibility and take control of our lives. Every month ended with
my dad chasing the life insurance person out of the driveway as the kids
cheered Dad on from the sidelines. Premature death is not a popular subject . . . a 100 percent success ratio is.

Always insure the machine that creates the money. The following
are the rules for buying life insurance:

**1. Opt for the best buy.** If you know exactly how much insurance
you want to purchase, pick up the phone and call your local agent or identify an agency that sells directly to the public. If you don't need any advice, it's easy to call:[2]

| | |
|---|---|
| • Direct quote | 800-845-3853 |
| • Quick quote | 800-867-2404 |
| • Best quote | 800-896-8006 |
| • America's Life Insurance Corporation | 800-255-9678 |
| • First TransAmerica Life Insurance Company | 800-544-0506 |
| • John Alden Insurance Company | 800-435-7969 |

**2. Buy adequate coverage.** There are a lot of formulas in the marketplace to help you determine the amount of coverage you need and it's
as easy as multiplying 10 times your annual income. If you make
$30,000, you would need $300,000 worth of life insurance. Personal insurance: you want to have a life insurance death benefit large enough so
that when it's combined with your other investments, the members of
your family will be able to live off of the income for the rest of their lives
without sacrificing their living standards. For example, if you only have
$50,000 in your retirement plan, $20,000 in your personal mutual fund

---

2.This does not constitute all sources of quote sources.

account, and $5,000 of cash reserves in the bank, for a total of $75,000, then it's easy to calculate that $75,000 will generate $5,600 per year if your family lives off the interest at 8 percent.

$$\begin{array}{r} \$75,000 \\ \times\,8\% \\ \hline \$5,600/\text{year} \end{array}$$

If you're currently earning $100,000 then your family needs to replace your $100,000 worth of income. Living off of $5,600 will absolutely force everybody to submit employment applications at a pancake house. The challenges arise when you have a spouse that may not be adequately prepared to go into the workforce immediately and replace your lost income. Let's use our multiple of 10 times your income, which would give us an insurance benefit of $1 million. Add that $1 million to the $75,000 you currently have in your retirement plan, mutual funds, and your cash reserves, and you now have $1,075,000. At the rate of 8 percent, this will provide $85,600 per year, replacing your income.

*Family Income =*
$$\begin{array}{l} \$1,000,000 \ \text{Death benefit} \\ +\ \ \$75,000 \ \text{Investments} \\ \hline \$1,075,000 \\ \qquad\quad \times\,8\% \\ \hline \textbf{\$85,600 annually} \end{array}$$

**3. If you find a better policy . . . buy it!** Times have changed and so have your policies and their costs. You never want to give in easily and liquidate an old policy because, generally speaking, you'll pay surrender charges and literally throw away money that you've already paid in to make that policy work. So, before you are enticed by these new policies, check the facts and compare numbers. If you find a better policy that won't take you a decade or two to recover the money you'll be losing from your canceled policy, then go ahead and purchase it after getting an impartial second opinion. Always compare policies with their mortality charges and administrative fees.

## Key-Person Business Life Insurance

Personal life insurance exists for the creation of tax-free funds for the remaining family members to replace the income of the deceased breadwinner. Everyone should own at least two different life insurance policies: *key-person life insurance* and *personal life insurance.* Key-person life insurance is purchased by the corporation or your sole proprietorship business on the owner of the company (you). In this way, if anything happens to the owner of the company, there will be money in the company to guide it through the transition phase until the new owner is found or the company is sold.

The most valuable asset in your business is the machine that creates the money, which is you. If someone steals your car, or a fire burns down your office and all your equipment, all of those assets are replaceable. You are not.

The skills you bring to the business, your contacts and experience, and your ability to effectuate a plan to make your business successful are your most valuable business assets.

Do you have 10 years of experience or do you have 1 year of experience 10 times?

All of the contacts and experience you bring to the table you now want to turn into profits. How do you place a value on your skills, ability, integrity, and personality? Estimate your revenue-generating ability on an annual basis, multiply it by five years, and that number will give you a reasonable amount. For example, if your income-generating ability is $75,000 per year times five years, that's $375,000. This would be a reasonable amount of life insurance to protect your business in the event of your untimely death. This money would provide the business with five years' worth of assets to replace your annual income of $75,000. During this period, your spouse or partner may wish to bring another person in to run the business or make the decision to run that business themselves. It could take approximately five years to get to the level of competency to replace your expertise.

As you'll learn, death is not the most threatening hardship that could affect your business. You have a greater chance of becoming disabled for more than 90 days during your career than you do of dying. You'll see later how disability life insurance should become an integral part of your Security Bucket #1.

## Short-Term or Long-Term Coverage

The main reason to buy life insurance is to cover an obligation or replace the regular income, as we've just discussed. If for whatever reason you need short-term coverage for five years or less, pay particular attention to the following illustration. What you'll find out is that there is a crossover point (the point in time where an annual renewable term coverage increases in cost each year and becomes more expensive than long-term insurance) at approximately year five on an annual renewable term insurance policy. Annual renewable means premiums that continue to go up on an annual basis as the policy is renewed. A 10- or 20-year level premium (meaning that premiums stay level for a specified period of years) is cheaper over longer periods of time. As you can see from the illustration below, when shopping for life insurance for a time or "term" of less than 10 years, you're better off purchasing the annually renewable policy. If you want to hold the policy longer, up to 10 or even 20 years, then you should purchase a 20-year level term policy or a whole or universal life policy.

Premium Comparisons For Various Policies
$500,000 Death Benefit
Insurance Cost Comparison: 40-Year-Old Male, Preferred,
Good Health, Nonsmoker

| Type of Policy | 20-Year Average Annual Premium | Total Premiums after 20 Years | Cash Value Year 20 |
|---|---|---|---|
| 1. Annual renewable term policy[a] | $1,413 | $ 28,260 | 0 |
| 2. 10-year level term policy[b] | $ 877 | $ 17,550 | 0 |
| 3. 20-year level term policy[c] | $ 835 | $ 16,700 | 0 |
| 4. Universal life policy | $2,880 | $ 57,600[d] | $ 70,957[e] |
| 5. Whole life policy | $7,285 | $145,700 | $146,500 |

[a] On 1/1/97, term rates will increase with the new guidelines being instituted that require companies selling term insurance to put up three times the amount of reserves to cover claims. This will increase the term costs.

[b] Level premiums guaranteed for 10 years.

[c] Level premiums guaranteed for 20 years.

[d] Values shown are guaranteed assuming all contract premiums are paid, no dividends are paid, and no loans or surrenders are made.

[e] Based on 7 percent projected interest rates. Projections based on current mortality charges, fees, and interest rates, which are all subject to change.

## Term Life Insurance

Term insurance is covered for a definite period of time, which translates into a specific number of years owned. The term may be for 1, 10, or 20 years. Generally, it is the cheapest type of life insurance available and the death benefit is paid upon the death of the insured when it occurs during the term of the contract.

If you purchase a 10-year term insurance policy, generally you would have the option to renew that same policy for an additional term.

A level term policy is designed for the premium to stay level for the entire length of the policy term. On the other hand, annually renewable term policies generally increase on a year-to-year basis. Depending on the situation, these policies are generally cheaper in the early years, at which point, if you decide to keep these policies for longer periods of time, it is cheaper to purchase a level-term policy. In the later years of your life, term insurance contracts can become very expensive and may be prohibitive based on cost. As you've seen in the preceding illustration, there is no cash value that accumulates in your term policy.

## Universal Life Insurance

Universal life insurance policies came about as a result of the high interest rates during the late 70s. Many people in their 40s and 50s never purchased universal life insurance policies because the interest rates the policies paid were tied to the portfolio returns that the insurance companies were receiving, less expenses and fees from the investment portfolios managed by the insurance companies. Generally, the insurance companies paid a rate of interest that changed every 12 months based on the performance of the investment portfolio. All companies have a guaranteed minimum interest rate, which is approximately 4 percent to 4½ percent.

Universal life policies separate the death benefit and cash value. Based upon interest rates paid on the policy, universal life could be the cheapest form of insurance you could own over the long term. The cash value is the property of the policy owner and may be withdrawn in a taxable manner or, utilizing the "borrowing provision," the policy's cash value may be borrowed by the policy owner in a tax advantaged manner for personal consumption. Individuals utilize these tax-advantages via the borrowing privilege to enhance retirement income, offset college costs, and so on. You should consult with a professional agent for the rules, regulations, and other illustrations.

## Whole Life Insurance

The premiums of the whole life insurance policy are level and guaranteed for the life of the entire contract. The insurance company will provide you with an illustration based upon your age, health, and the percentage of death benefits you request. The premiums are to be paid each and every year for the life of the policy. You also will find personal portfolios that limit your premiums to a specific number of years. In a whole life policy, you will always know the exact cost of the policy and, similar to a universal life policy, you will accumulate cash that is the property of the policy owner. The policy owner retains access to this cash value in the future by withdrawing cash in a taxable manner or utilizing the borrowing provision and borrowing cash in a tax-advantaged manner.

If you desire insurance for a lifetime or greater than the 20-year term limit (the maximum number of years insurance companies will write a term policy), then you need to purchase a variable life, universal life, or whole life policy.

## When You Should Replace Old Policies

**1.** In 1996, the life expectancy is 74 years for males and 78 years for females. With the cost of life insurance spread out based on your life expectancy, it's easy to see why life insurance policies are becoming more competitive than ever before. Term insurance policies are the most competitive based on the current marketplace. With mortality costs decreasing, most new policies could be cheaper than your old policy. In other words, the underlying fees are coming down and the insurance companies are competitively passing along those savings.

**2.** Inflation, higher fees, and possibly lower rates on old policies may have made them inadequate. Just think about a $100,000 life insurance policy purchased in 1963. After the erosion of inflation on that $100,000 death benefit, you would have actual real buying power today of $21,000. Make sure you reevaluate your insurance needs over each ensuing 10-year period of time so that, in the event of death, your family won't be living on the lower purchasing power of a death benefit you purchased 20 years ago.

**3.** Most families need additional insurance and don't think they can afford it until they price today's new competitive rates.

**4.** If you have multiple policies, look at combining those policies into new lower-rate policies. Sometimes you'll find that a business owner or the head of the household has accumulated two, three, and even four different policies during his or her lifetime. Some of these policies go back to World War II. I highly recommend having these policies evaluated by an expert. I've reviewed insurance policies and have been able to multiply the value of many of the policies and reduce the premiums. Find an honest agent who will let you know when you are better off keeping your old policy rather than going through the expense of buying a new policy.

**5.** If you purchased cash value policies when interest rates were higher in the early 80s, paying 9 percent–12 percent, then you must have these policies reviewed now. A lot of those older policies were written based on higher interest rate assumptions. In other words when you paid money into your policy each year, it netted out the annual fees, leaving the net cash value in the policy. This cash value (your money) grew at various rates of return each year. If these policies were sold and projected out at the higher interest rates and currently lower interest rates are being paid, your policy could self-destruct because your money isn't growing fast enough at today's lower interest rates to stay ahead of the escalating fees in the later years of the contract.

But keep in mind, never cancel an old policy until a new one has been approved, put in place, and paid for so that you're never left without coverage. If you eliminate your old coverage and you're turned down by the new company because of some health problem you didn't know about, you'd be left without coverage. Another reason to always keep your old policy in spite of the expense is if you are in bad health or you are uninsurable. In this case, the policy may appear expensive to you, but it may be the only insurance you are ever able to obtain.

## INCOME PROTECTION

How long could you live on your savings if your health prevented you from going to work tomorrow? Out of 1,000 people, the likelihood of becoming disabled for at least 90 days before age 65 is shown below.

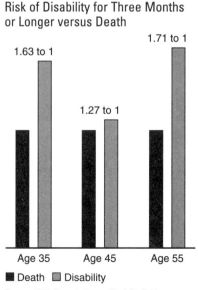

Risk of Disability for Three Months or Longer versus Death

Source: 1986 Commissioners Disability Table.

This illustration shows that the chances are far greater than most people realize that the machine that creates the money will stop for at least 90 days during its working career. It only makes sense to insure the machine that creates the money, since we insure everything else in our lives. Not only that, but the average duration of a disability that lasts over 90 days is shown below.

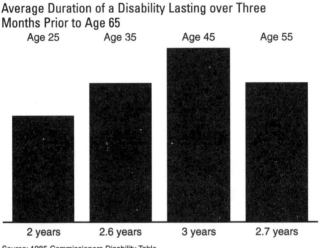

Average Duration of a Disability Lasting over Three Months Prior to Age 65

Source: 1985 Commissioners Disability Table.

If you haven't built a business either out of your home or in your career that provides residual income, then it's absolutely critical that you provide income replacement in the event of an interruption of your own income. Disability insurance won't make you money, but it will replace a portion of your lost income if you become disabled.

## MAKE MONEY OFF YOUR MORTGAGE

How can you take the biggest debt that 50 percent of the adult population will incur during its lifetime and cut the payment up to 50 percent, putting tens and even hundreds of thousands of dollars back in your pocket? Speed up your mortgage payments?

Let's start by gaining a quick understanding of what your mortgage payment actually consists of. Let's assume you have a $100,000 mortgage. If you look closely at your amortization schedule (variable rate loans have no amortization schedule because of fluctuations in interest rates), you'll see how much of your payment goes toward interest and how much goes toward the principal. For example, a $1,000 payment would be $804.62 of interest and $54.62 of principal. Let's review a typical amortization schedule:

*Basic Loan Information*

| | | | |
|---|---|---|---|
| Amount | $100,000.00 | Annual interest rate | 9.00% |
| Beginning of loan | 1/1/97 | Length of loan, years | 30 |

*Payment Information*

| | | | |
|---|---|---|---|
| Total payments | **360** | Calculated Payment | **$804.62** |
| Payments per year | 12 | | |

*Summary Information*

| | | | |
|---|---|---|---|
| Total paid | **($289,664.17)** | Interest paid | **($189,664.17)** |

| Pmnt # | Start of Period | Annual Interest Rate | Scheduled Balance | Actual Balance | Scheduled Payment | Interest Portion | Principal Portion |
|---|---|---|---|---|---|---|---|
| 1 | Jan | 9.00% | 100,000.00 | 100,000.00 | (804.62) | (750.00) | (54.62) |
| 2 | Feb | 9.00% | 99,945.38 | 99,945.38 | (804.62) | (749.59) | (55.03) |
| 3 | March | 9.00% | 99,890.35 | 99,890.35 | (804.62) | (749.18) | (55.45) |
| 4 | April | 9.00% | 99,834.90 | 99,834.90 | (804.62) | (748.76) | (55.86) |
| 5 | May | 9.00% | 99,779.04 | 99,779.04 | (804.62) | (748.34) | (56.28) |

In the example above, look at your interest (the amount you're paying for your loan) and your principal (the amount of equity you're building each month) and you'll see that with each $804.62 monthly payment, your actual ownership is minimal. Step outside the front door of your home and stare at your $55 mailbox, which is approximately what you own after your first $804.62 monthly payment. If you look clearly at the principal and interest columns of January, February, and March, you'll see that the bulk of your payment every month goes toward payment of debt interest but not equity building in your own home. The bank owns the bulk of the house and you're paying a hefty rate of interest to own a very tiny piece of your home each month. How many years do you think it takes for the principal to equal the interest payment? Up to 22.4 years! A typical $100,000 home will cost almost three times that when you add up all the interest at the end of 30 years. In other words, a $100,000 home will cost almost $300,000. Who do you think is making more money? You or the bank?

## SIMPLE SOLUTIONS

My concept is very simple. If you have a fixed-rate loan, call up your mortgage company and ask for an amortization schedule, which will break out what we have done in our above example. You will then make your monthly payment of $804.62 and look on your amortization schedule for the next month's principal payment. In our case, the February payment is $55.03. You would pay your January payment of $804.62 and next month's principal payment of $55.03 for a total payment of $859.65. If you follow this process and continue to make the following month's principal payment with each payment you make, you will never have to make the corresponding month's interest payment. In our example, if you paid January's payment of $804.62 and the next month's principal payment of $55.03, you would never have to pay February's interest payment of $749.59. Now I know this sounds too good to be true, but just think what the interest would be on $55 if you financed that amount over the next 29 years and 11 months. By prepaying principal, you are knocking down your debt on a monthly basis and saving as much as 29 years and 11 months of interest on your first prepayment. Now for those of you who have a variable rate mortgage, there's no amortization schedule available, so you can't designate how much extra principal you want to pay each month. Whether you're on a fixed rate or a variable rate mortgage, just be sure your extra principal payment is paying down the principal each month.

The bottom line: (1) pay off a 30-year loan in 19 to 23 years depending on the loan value; (2) be absolutely mortgage-debt free; and (3) continue your $804.62 payment into your own personal investment account. You choose: Would you rather have a $100,000 home costing almost $300,000 at the end of 30 years under a typical 30-year mortgage plan or a 30-year mortgage paid off in 22.4 years, leaving you completely mortgage-debt free and with an additional $100,685 of cash in investments at your disposal at the end of 30 years?

## WORKING MONEY

I've always believed that the masses would more effectively manage their money if somebody explained it to them in a crystal clear format that was easy and encouraged them to take action. Eliminate the jargon of Wall Street, the hype and hustlers and get-rich-quick schemes that seem to fill our mailboxes and lay out a plain no-nonsense approach for managing money for both short-term and long-term appreciation. In this chapter, you've come to understand clearly that there is no one more important in your wealth accumulation plan than the person that creates the money.

While we're on our road to accumulate assets to attain financial freedom, we need to make doubly sure that in the event we become disabled for 90 days or more, we have an income replacement program in place so that we don't have to drain our existing assets down to the embarrassment level.

You've learned that the principle of wealth creation is built around the model that there is a strategy to counteract every major expense. Begin immediately and reduce credit card rates up to 50 percent, saving approximately $200 per year; never pay the minimum credit card payment and save literally thousands on a $2,000 credit card balance; avoid low-paying bank money funds paying an average 2.6 percent and checking accounts paying zero percent on your money and move your assets to the top money market funds and increase your yield up to 100 percent; for long-term cash reserve assets, consider dividend-paying stocks with upside potential, as seen in our Texaco 38 percent total return example; and prepay your mortgage payment similar to credit cards and cut your 30-year mortgage to as little as 19–21 years and put hundreds of thousands back in your own personal account where it belongs. Finally, you have a 100 percent chance of dying, so why do it for free? Buy the right type of life insurance and leave a tax-free legacy you can be proud of.

# Strategy #7: Change the Way You Approach Financial Planning

Money has no loyalty:
It always seeks its best employment.

## CONTROLLING THE FLOW OF MONEY

It's impossible to save too much money for retirement. With most investments, you pay taxes on the annual earnings and capital gains taxes on profits, reducing your return. For example, $50,000 invested at 8 percent taxable over 20 years, assuming a 28 percent tax bracket, grows to $153,249. That same investment made on a tax-deferred basis could grow to $233,047. If your goal is to accumulate as much money for retirement as possible and do it in the shortest period of time, then it's important to understand how tax-deferred investing will set you free. All of your money continues to work for you over the years to earn you more money, deferring all taxes until you decide to withdraw it. The tax savings continue to be invested on an annual basis and exponentially multiply the growth of your future family net worth.

The information I've shared with you thus far should make you start to question the way you earn a living. To review:

- We are entering a period of profound change regarding the way people approach business, resulting in one of the greatest mass movements in the history of the United States in over 200 years.
- The new era of collaborative economics signifies a level playing field for anyone, without prejudice or partiality.
- The middleman who gets closer to the customer makes the most money.
- The IRS will literally subsidize your business with tax benefits until you're so successful you have no choice but to pay taxes.
- The money machine strategy will help you create a family fortune three times faster, creating more six-figure incomes and millionaires than in any other decade in history.

Learning how to uncover your extraordinary talents and position yourself to profit handsomely in the years ahead is only half of the equation. As you expand your business savvy and the scope of your investing, you need to aggressively grasp the strategies and secrets that will increase the *flow of money* at your control.

I grew up in a big Italian family with a lot of love and little money. I rode my bike at an early age across the city line to go to school in the next town. It was then that I noticed that many of those people had more expensive homes and newer cars, took more lavish vacations, and just plain had more money. Kids from our neighborhood would continue to look at people as they drove by in their better cars, walked around in their finer clothes, or went inside their newer homes, and without saying a word, the unwritten sentiment that you picked up on was, "Money is for those *other people.*" As a 12-year-old boy, riding my bike through those finer neighborhoods on my way back home each day, I came to the conclusion that the only difference between my dad, who would work longer and harder to get the job done, and my good friend's dad from the finer uptown neighborhood was that one had access to greater choices at an earlier point in his life. If my dad had had access to the same information and the same opportunities, he might have made better choices at an earlier point in his life. It took that simple thinking to bring home the fact that I could be as good as anybody from any background or any income level as long as I taught myself the rules to the game of money.

## DECLINING DOLLARS AND INCREASING PRICES

Those rules have become increasingly important, if you consider how much the value of the dollar has fluctuated over the last few decades. Consider the following statistics:

1. The average worker's salary has risen sharply over the past three decades. But when you adjust for inflation, the average hourly wage actually has dropped since 1973. According to the Economic Report of the President dated February 1995, in 1994, the average hourly wage was $11.12. Adjusted for inflation, that number was $7.40 of real buying power. Contrast that to approximately $8.00 in 1975.[1]

2. Based on the current price index, the value of the dollar that bought $1 worth of goods in 1963 fell to a real buying power of 21¢ in 1993 when adjusted for inflation.[2]

3. Based on a 5 percent inflation rate, the ravages of inflation over a 25-year period of time will drive the $1.35 loaf of bread to $4.57; five pounds of potatoes at $1.49 to $5.04; a half gallon of milk at $1.40 to $4.74; and a three-bedroom home valued at $145,000 to over $490,000.

How Much Money Will I Need?

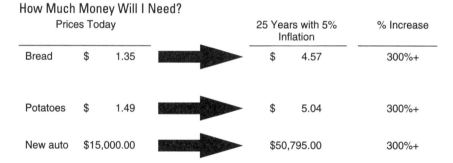

| | Prices Today | | 25 Years with 5% Inflation | % Increase |
|---|---|---|---|---|
| Bread | $ | 1.35 | $    4.57 | 300%+ |
| Potatoes | $ | 1.49 | $    5.04 | 300%+ |
| New auto | $15,000.00 | | $50,795.00 | 300%+ |

With the real buying power of inflation-adjusted hourly wages declining, the real buying power of the dollar declining, and prices rising to offset the ravages of inflation, it becomes critically important that those interested in maintaining and enhancing their standard of living in the future develop an absolutely clear understanding of this game called money.

1. Gary Bisgaitis, *USA Today*.
2. As determined by a monthly survey of the U.S. Bureau of Labor Statistics.

Can you imagine getting into a game where you didn't understand the rules? Of course not. Most likely, 9 times out of 10, you'd lose. If you're going to get into a game that absolutely affects your life, your family, your attitude, and your emotions, then you ought to buckle your seat belt, shift your mind into overdrive, and develop a clear understanding of the strategies that will put you in the driver's seat and let you determine your destination.

The fact is: Every one of us has the potential to feed our minds so that we can multiply our output. We can leverage our minds by accelerating our information and education in order to reach to whatever lofty levels we care to dream. The first strategy that I learned is to think of myself in terms of an income-producing machine. It would only make sense that my job is to go out and create as much income as possible, spend less than I make, and invest the difference in another machine that will ultimately replace me.

Once your machine begins to fill up with money, your goal is very straightforward: Replace the machine that created the money, which is yourself. All this means is that, once you have enough money to live off the interest, you have, in effect, replaced yourself. Then the machine can continue to work every minute of the day, seven days a week, four weeks a month, twelve months a year, and on and on. That's a machine that never sleeps and its output will be determined only by your investment ability.

The idea is to fill up your money machine as quickly as possible. In the early months and years, people become disenchanted and quit because when $1 doubles it only equals $2, $2 doubles to $4, $4 to $8, and $8 to $16, and so forth. But eventually the money machine reaches exponential growth and you realize you have $5,000 doubling to $10,000, $10,000 doubling to $20,000, $20,000 to $40,000, $40,000 to $80,000, and $80,000 to $160,000, and so on. The secret is to persevere in your journey until you reach exponential growth.

## THE INVESTMENT MIDDLEMAN SHOULD BE REPLACED

The second strategy, which will absolutely produce a reversal in your thinking, is one that I learned very early on. When you go down to the bank to deposit your money into a savings account or a money market account, it will pay you approximately 4 percent per annum or whatever the competitive rate is at that time. As I deposited my money into a savings account, money market account, or other savings vehicle, it always interested me what a *"no-brainer"* choice I had made. What were my alternatives? A cigar box? At the same time, I also became increasingly inquisitive as to what the bank did with my money. With a little more research, I found out that after assuring me a *reasonable* rate of return such as 4 percent, the bank would turn around and loan it out for a home mortgage at anywhere from 7–10 percent (depending on the current rate) or for a personal loan at 12 percent, or issue credit card debt at 15–19 percent. What a concept. In the old neighborhood, they called this loan sharking, but at the bank it was legitimate business.

It didn't take long to figure out I was the low man on the totem pole. Now, I was starting to get a feel for how the money game works, and I discovered that if I could only cut out the middleman in the investment game and go directly to the higher earning investments, I could increase my return 25–100 percent immediately.

Always Eliminate the Investment Middleman

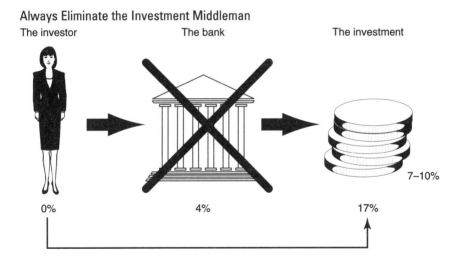

As time progressed, I also found out how difficult it was to get money out of a bank when you wanted a loan. And any of us who have tried to get a loan when we really needed one have figured out that it's virtually impossible. Of course, when you make so much money that you don't need the loan, they'll fall all over themselves to try and give you one. What you'll learn in the remaining chapters of this book is how to bypass the middleman and literally put tens of thousands—if not hundreds of thousands—of dollars in your pocket using slight edge strategies. Knowledge helps create and perpetuate wealth.

## THE SECOND GREATEST STORY EVER TOLD

The third and final strategy to use in developing your financial plan is what I call the Bucket Story. It's absolutely the most important strategy you'll ever learn to create financial freedom.

This is a story I've taught for over 10 years. I've taught it to the struggling 25 year old with seven credit cards totally awash in debt, as well as to corporate executives, multimillionaires, and everyone in between.

### Secrets of Wealth Accumulation Planning: The Bucket Story

Security Bucket #1 will earn you the right to invest into your Growth Investment Bucket, which is Bucket #2. When you fill Bucket #2 and obtain financial independence, your dollars will overflow into your Dream Bucket, Bucket #3. Result: The opportunity and right to purchase the Dream Bucket items that you've always aspired to and deserve.

**Security Bucket #1**
*Heighten your basic needs and peace of mind*

1. Home
2. Life insurance
3. Disability insurance
4. College education funding
5. Pension plans
6. 6–12 months of cash reserves in bank

*As each bucket fills, the overflow fills the next one.*

**Risk Bucket #2**
*Your financial independence*

1. Stocks/bonds
2. Mutual funds
3. Tax lien certificates
4. Second mortgages
5. Real estate

**Dream Bucket #3**
*Once you've filled Bucket #2, you've again EARNED THE RIGHT to place dollars into your Dream Bucket.*

1. Race horses
2. Resorts
3. Aircraft
4. Race cars

## Step 1: Bulletproof Your Assets

Bucket #1 is your *security bucket*. If you're just getting started, have accumulated assets during your lifetime, or have already achieved wealth during your life, now is the time to realign your financial roadmap. Before you do anything else in your life, you need to go back to Bucket #1 and begin implementing or realigning your security bucket by combining the idea of a home-based business with the management of your personal financial affairs. Your security bucket should contain the following: separate business and personal checking accounts; separate business and personal credit cards; funds to help you finance your own home, if you haven't already done so; six months' personal cash reserve; education funds for your children, business, and personal life; disability insurance; and your retirement plan.

If you're like me, you started out differently. I always thought the greatest path to financial freedom was absolute risk, that is, maximizing my dollars in a way that would return the greatest amount of money. The only problem with this happy-go-lucky approach is that if you lose your money, you could lose your assets and, if you have obligations such as family, children, or business debt, this could prove disastrous. My definition of embarrassment is showing up at home with more bills than money and 10 more days left in the month.

### Feed Your Family, Not Your Ego

At the age of 16, I started tracking stocks in my quest to get ahead. My first thought was to actually go out and take risks to get the greatest return for my money. I saved over $1,000 and at the same time tracked five stocks: Mostek Corporation, National Semiconductor Corporation, Motorola, Intel Corporation, and Texas Instruments. Back in 1973, all of these stocks happened to be computer-chip-related companies at the brink of the boom in the computer industry.

I purchased a book on logarithmic graphing of stocks, inspired by my Uncle Mike, who worked in the computer chip industry. It seemed pretty simple to a novice's eye. If you follow stocks for a period of time and graph their movement and price, they all seem to follow some type of pattern. Semiconductor stocks or cyclical stocks generally move up and down in a recognizable pattern throughout their cycles. The simple philosophy I followed was to understand the average high and the average low of these stocks, and try to purchase them at the low point in their cycles.

My first purchase was National Semiconductor stock, and after following it for over a year and tracking it on my daily and weekly graph, I decided that $12 was a good price and the low point in its cycle. I shuttled myself down to the local brokerage firm on my way to work during the summer before my first year of college. Initially mistaken for the local paper boy, when the firm discovered I was holding $1,000 cash in my front pocket, I was ushered in to the manager's office, who happened to be the first one to arrive that morning. He attempted to talk me out of my purchase, which was virtually impossible because I had just spent a year researching the first investment of my entire life and I had *conviction based on knowledge.* I went ahead and purchased $1,000 of National Semiconductor at $12 a share and I happily went along in my jeans and t-shirt to my summer job. Each day I would stop by the brokerage firm and punch in the symbol "NSM" to see what the price of National Semiconductor was that day. Much to my surprise, National Semiconductor didn't go up but continued to go down—only to bottom out at $6 per share. Based on what I had read, if I had additional money I would have purchased additional shares in National Semiconductor. The brokers told me to sell my stock, lick my wounds, take my money, and run. I continued to persist based on my convictions. Lo and behold, National Semiconductor started one of the biggest growth spurts in its history, catapulting to new highs. The stock split 2 times between 1970 and 1973—2 for 1 in February 1971 and 3 for 1 in January 1974.

## Financial Certainty

Developing a winning attitude is critically important in this story, but developing a reality attitude will take you even further in your financial life. I could have lost my money or caved in and cashed out at $6 per share because of lack of conviction or conviction that I had made a bad purchase. Just imagine the feeling of embarrassment if I had no money in my Security Bucket #1 with a family to support, possibly children to raise, and debts waiting to be paid. Out of this thought process, I became determined to not only create certainty in my personal life but also embark upon a journey that would create security in my financial life, while at the same time providing me with higher returns for my calculated investment risks.

What if I could take generally boring security bucket expenses and turn them into investments that would pay me back throughout my lifetime? Not only did this idea get me more excited about investing in

Bucket #1 and creating the security I never had, but it made me think about the prospects of turning expenses into profit centers. Just imagine turning boring expenses, such as life insurance and home mortgages, into newly developed profit centers. Instead of just paying these bills every month, I could use innovative strategies to turn these expenses into future income. Add multiple sources of income (MSIs) and you create the success formula I call *ultimate leverage.*

## Step 2: Earn the Right to Risk

Once you turn your expenses into profit centers as well as create your MSIs in Bucket #1, you earn the right to invest in Risk Bucket #2. Bucket #2 contains your risk investments in common stocks, bonds, real estate, and a variety of other investments for growth. This is the money that spilled over after you fully funded Bucket #1. Your risk bucket contains exactly that—*risk assets.* These are assets that fluctuate on a regular basis and will ultimately bring you the greatest return. Remember how I told you to think of yourself as an income-producing machine where you spend less than you make and invest the difference in an investment machine that will ultimately replace you? If you look closely, you'll see in the accompanying table exactly how much money you need to accumulate, invested at 7 percent, in order to replace your current income.

### How Much Critical Mass Do You Need to Achieve to Replace Your Annual Income?

| Critical Mass | Annual Income (7%) | Monthly Income |
|---|---|---|
| $    100,000 | $      7,000 | $       583 |
| $    250,000 | $    17,500 | $    1,458 |
| $    500,000 | $    35,000 | $    2,916 |
| $    750,000 | $    52,500 | $    4,375 |
| $1,000,000 | $    70,000 | $    5,833 |
| $1,250,000 | $    87,500 | $    7,291 |
| $1,500,000 | $ 105,000 | $    8,750 |
| $1,750,000 | $ 122,500 | $ 10,208 |
| $2,000,000 | $ 140,000 | $ 11,666 |
| $2,250,000 | $ 157,500 | $ 13,125 |
| $2,500,000 | $ 175,000 | $ 14,583 |
| $4,000,000 | $ 280,000 | $ 23,333 |
| $5,000,000 | $ 350,000 | $ 29,166 |

Note: These figures haven't taken into consideration your tax bracket. It is estimated you will need 70 percent of your income for a safe retirement.

## Step 3: Live Your Dreams

Once you've accumulated enough critical mass in Security Bucket #1 and Risk Bucket #2 (that is, enough to replace your income and pay off your debts), you've *earned the right* to overflow your money into Dream Bucket #3. Your dream bucket includes all of those exotic cars, second or third homes, and toys, as I'll call them, that are not a must to own, but that you've earned the right to own.

The moral of the story is that you've got to take immediate control of your financial future. There is nothing more important that you'll gain from our time together than the total belief that now more than ever the roadmap is clear and your time is now. You can become a master of your destiny from this day forward. Whether you're a chief executive officer, a chairman of a major corporation, a lawyer, a physician, or just someone getting started and making your first investment, the tools to master your destiny have never been more compelling.

## REALLOCATE YOUR PROFITS

Your successful implementation of these strategies will ultimately lead to your dream purchases by filling Dream Bucket #3. Remember, when you cash in and make big profits in Risk Bucket #2, reallocate your profits as follows:

1. Put one-third of your money back into Security Bucket #1.
2. Put one-third of your money back into Risk Bucket #2.
3. Take the remainder (if you choose this option) and place up to one-third in your Dream Bucket #3.

Enjoy your victory . . . you deserve it!

## NOTHING BUT THE FACTS

I don't know how many times I've heard stories of a phenomenal Wall Street whiz or real estate tycoon who continued to parlay his or her money only to lose everything because of one miscalculation. These are people who have worked 60 to 80 hours a week for years in the hopes that they would someday be free but instead ended up broke. Grasp the success you've attained, reinvest your assets for growth, and always enjoy your success in the present.

With so many companies, services, and professionals offering advice, it's no wonder that the selection of insurance products has come down to a one-on-one relationship with your agent. If you're not completely attuned to the facts, figures, and details of how these products actually work, then do yourself a favor that could save you or make you tens of thousands of dollars . . . get professional help now!

There are no secrets; you just need a plan. It's no surprise to any of us that we can see a difference of tens and even hundreds of thousands of dollars invested on a tax-deferred basis, as interest rises quickly. *Spend less than you make and invest the majority of the difference in tax-deferred vehicles that will grow your assets on an annual basis without the destructive reduction of annual capital gains taxes.* Why would anyone consider allowing up to 50 percent of their money, depending on your individual tax bracket, to disappear every single year in an investment portfolio that you've worked so hard to earn? Multiply your assets—and ultimately your income—up to 300 percent faster over time by utilizing fixed-income annuities for your conservative long-term cash reserve assets and tax-deferred variable annuities for your long-term growth-oriented assets, and consider variable life insurance with mutual funds as a long-term family planning and tax reduction vehicle for future retirement income. When it comes to tax-deferred investing, a little knowledge could mean the difference in the standard of life you live 20, 30, or even 40 years from now.

# Strategy #8: Invest in Insurance Products and Reap Numerous Tax Advantages

**Who Should Consider Investing in Tax Advantaged Products?**

Investors who:

1. Are in a high combined federal/state tax bracket.
2. Have seen their total tax bill increase dramatically because of lost personal deductions.
3. Rely on investments as their primary source of income.
4. Have investment portfolios that contain only taxable investments.
5. Are currently earning low rates from their investments.
6. Have reached the limit on contributions to retirement plans.
7. Are just starting to invest.

## A BRIEF EXPLANATION ABOUT ANNUITIES

Technically speaking, annuities are a kind of insurance, although their primary function is not one of protection. Unlike term insurance or other types of life insurance, you do not have to die to collect your money. In other words, a tax-deferred annuity sponsored by a life insurance annuity company gives you an investment that will compound dollars free from taxes on any interest, dividends, or capital gains until such time as you decide to receive payments. Then and only then will you pay taxes on the earnings, *never on your principal.*

Annuities come in two basic varieties. The most popular is a *fixed annuity,* something akin to a guaranteed money market or certificate of deposit, with the interest rate adjusted annually or locked in for a specified number of years. The other is the rapidly growing *variable annuity* product, in which your money is invested in a variety of stock and bond mutual funds with the performance based entirely on the performance of the mutual funds.

## Guaranteed Return Annuities (GRAs)—Fixed Annuities

Guaranteed rates, tax deferral, no up-front sales charge!

Guaranteed return annuities provide just what the name implies: a guaranteed rate of return for a specified period of time from three months to 10 years. You choose the period of time in which you would like to *"lock up"* your money, just like a certificate of deposit (CD) or Treasury bond. The insurance company will provide you with a guaranteed rate that usually is higher than other fixed-rate instruments in the same low-risk environment. The insurance company also will stand behind the investment with a 100 percent guarantee that you will never lose your principal or interest. *Your money is guaranteed against loss.*

Guaranteed return annuities offer the following:

1. **Tax Savings**—resulting from tax-deferred investment income.
2. **No Initial Sales Charge**—meaning that 100 percent of your purchase payments go to work for you immediately.
3. **Competitive Yields**—GRAs offer the most competitive rates of all safe money alternatives, often higher than CDs or Treasury notes, for example.
4. **10 Percent Free Withdrawal Right**—after a purchase payment has been in the contract for one year, up to 10 percent of that amount may be withdrawn *free of charge* each year thereafter. Most, but not all, annuities offer this feature.
5. **No 1099s and No Probate.**

The guaranteed return annuity could be the most effective safe-money haven for conservative investment dollars. Your money grows safely with your prudent selection of the strongest and highest-rated insurance companies. Virtually all annuity companies have surrender charges during the contract life that decrease over time until they reach zero. The surrender penalty is the amount charged for early withdrawal of your money before the contract period is up (i.e., 5 percent in year 1, 4 percent in year 2, etc.). There is no surrender charge with the 10 percent annual withdrawal provision. After two to three years, the surrender charge could be less than the 50 percent penalty generally charged on CDs.

**Increase Your Future Income 18 Percent**

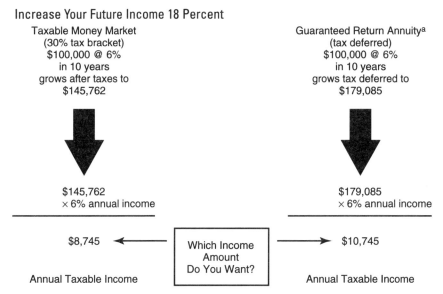

Taxable Money Market
(30% tax bracket)
$100,000 @ 6%
in 10 years
grows after taxes to
$145,762

Guaranteed Return Annuity[a]
(tax deferred)
$100,000 @ 6%
in 10 years
grows tax deferred to
$179,085

$145,762
× 6% annual income

$179,085
× 6% annual income

$8,745 ← Which Income Amount Do You Want? → $10,745

Annual Taxable Income

Annual Taxable Income

Notes: Assumptions: Taxable money market: 6 percent; Annuity: 6 percent; Tax bracket: 36 percent; Investment: $100,000.

[a] Generally pay higher.

---

**THE CHOICE IS YOURS! Sample: 10 Annuity Choices**

1. John Alden
2. Pacific Mutual
3. Transamerica Life and Annuity
4. USG Annuity and Life
5. General Assurance

6. First Colony Life
7. American General Life
8. Alexander Hamilton
9. Investors Insurance Corporation
10. Jackson National Life

## Variable Annuities

Variable annuities combine the investment advantages of mutual funds and the power of tax deferral. Imagine an investment that blends the diversification and growth potential of up to 22 mutual funds from eight different mutual fund companies, the power of tax-deferred compounding, and the freedom to make investments whenever and for whatever amount you desire, for as long as you choose. This is the essence of a variable annuity.

Like guaranteed return annuities, variable annuities provide you with the substantial benefit of tax-deferred compounding of your assets during your lifetime. Unlike guaranteed return annuities, variable annuities will allow you to select mutual funds within the annuity contract, encompassing as many as 22 mutual funds managed by eight different mutual fund companies. In contrast to a fixed-rate guarantee ranging from 1 to 10 years, you now have the growth potential of some of your favorite mutual funds and the opportunity to achieve long-term growth of your investment assets on a tax-deferred basis.

The key feature to remember is that a variable annuity's return is totally dependent on the performance of the mutual funds over time. That performance is dependent upon your selection of the most appropriate funds to meet your needs and objectives.

Let's take a closer look at the variable annuity benefits:

1. Tax free switching between funds.
2. Tax deferral of any interest, dividends, or capital gains until withdrawal.
3. Your principal is guaranteed against loss in the event of your death.
4. "Separate accounts" are walled off from insurance company creditors.
5. You get the most out of your money upon withdrawal.

Tax Deferral Can Grow More Money

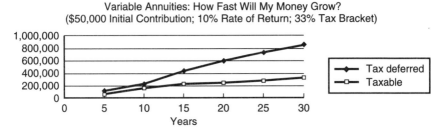

Variable Annuities: How Fast Will My Money Grow?
($50,000 Initial Contribution; 10% Rate of Return; 33% Tax Bracket)

### Tax Deferred Growth Can Lead to More Income

Turning Growth into Income

|  | Taxable | Tax Deferred |
|---|---|---|
| Accumulation | $349,867 | $872,470 |
| Rate of return | at 10% | at 10% |
| Annual earnings | $ 34,987 | $ 87,247 |
| Tax bracket | at 33% | at 33% |
| Annual income | $ 23,442 | $ 58,456 |

## TAX-FREE, COMMISSION-FREE SWITCHING BETWEEN FUNDS

This new generation of annuity allows you the ability to switch between up to 22 mutual funds from eight of America's leading mutual fund providers without incurring capital gains taxes.

Your fund family will include both international and domestic stock and bond funds, along with a guaranteed account and money market account. Based on your personal time horizon, risk tolerance, and market conditions, you will be able to select the appropriate funds to meet your goals and objectives, while at the same time maintaining the flexibility to move between funds without incurring charges or capital gains taxes. The diversification options featured within your annuity allow you a tremendous level of flexibility, tax deferral, and professional management. Switching between the funds is as easy as calling the toll-free 800 number. Of course, your advisor is available to help you determine your investment profile and help you select the most appropriate funds to meet your goals and objectives.

## TAX DEFERRAL OF ANY INTEREST, DIVIDENDS, OR CAPITAL GAINS UNTIL WITHDRAWAL

An annuity is a contract with a life insurance company that is often used as a retirement savings vehicle. Payments made to the annuity during the "accumulation phase" accumulate earnings on a tax-deferred basis.

That means you pay no taxes on your principal, no taxes on your interest, no taxes on your capital gains, and no taxes on the money you would have paid to the government, until you decide to withdraw the funds.

Add to this the fact that you can reinvest your interest, dividends, and capital gains in the meantime, which results in even greater investment returns by compounding your investment dollars until you decide to withdraw your money.

## THE EIGHTH WONDER OF THE WORLD—TAX-DEFERRED COMPOUNDING

Let me give you an example of how the compounding effect could change the way you invest from this day forward. If you put $100,000 into a taxable investment that averages a hypothetical 12 percent rate of return, compounded annually, after 10 years you would have $229,033, assuming a 28 percent tax bracket. Not so bad.

Let's say you put the same $100,000 into a variable annuity averaging the same 12 percent. After 10 years, you would have $310,585. In other words, you have created an additional $81,552 of critical mass. And that's in just 10 years. If you compounded the money for 20 years, you would put an extra $440,070 in your pocket. If you compounded your capital for 30 years, you would achieve a grand total of an extra $1,794,578 of critical mass.

## GUARANTEED AGAINST LOSS

One of the most unique and outstanding benefits of a variable annuity product is the fact that, in the event of your death, your heirs receive a guaranteed death benefit. Please keep in mind that unlike your life insurance policy, there are no medical or blood tests to take for a variable annuity. Nor are there any maximum or minimum investment amounts on an annual basis once your variable annuity is opened.

Now, back to the guarantee. Let's assume that you purchase a variable annuity for $100,000 by rolling over personal money that you previously had invested in mutual funds, stocks, or possibly your investment retirement account (IRA). Immediately afterwards, the markets become very volatile as economic uncertainty sweeps the marketplace and your funds decline 50 percent. The total market value of the securities in your variable annuity is now $50,000. In the event of your untimely death, the *annuity company* will pay your beneficiary the greater of the market value of your portfolio or your original investment (less withdrawals). In this case, *your heirs would be paid your original $100,000* and the insurance company would take a loss of $50,000 plus expenses.

On the other hand, how do we lock in the guarantee at a higher rate if, for instance, in five years, your account is now worth $500,000? In the event of a market crash, upon your death you would be adversely affected if your account was still only guaranteed for $100,000 of your original investment. Fortunately, many of the annuity companies raise the guaranteed death benefit every five years to minimize the effect of the potential disaster. Every five years, they "lock in" the new market value of your portfolio; that means your $500,000 would have been protected against your untimely death.

Guaranteed market values and mutual funds are quite a concept— and one that most investors will never know about!

## SEPARATE ACCOUNTS: INSURANCE COMPANY CREDITORS CAN'T TOUCH YOUR ASSETS

Money invested in your variable annuity is "walled off" or, technically speaking, placed in separate accounts so that it is not part of the general fund of the insurance company The bottom line to you is that your money is not available to creditors of the insurance company in the event that it has financial problems. This is a reassuring fact for those skeptical investors who feel that insurance companies may go the way of the S&Ls.

If, on the other hand, you place your money in the "fixed-account" mutual fund option of the variable annuity, your money is not considered part of the "separate account" and the above does not apply.

## GETTING THE MOST OUT OF YOUR MONEY AT WITHDRAWAL

There are fundamentally three major programs for the withdrawal of your money that are well known by the investment community. These are as follows:

**1. Lump-sum withdrawals.** Just as the name implies, you take the assets out of your tax-deferred variable annuity after age 59½ in one lump sum. You must wait until age 59½ to take money out without incurring a 10 percent IRS penalty. When you take the money out in one lump sum, you pay your ordinary income tax rate in that year. Taxes will be paid solely on the appreciation value of your investment and not on your principal.

**2. Annuitization.** You have the option with the annuity company to annuitize your contract over a period of time, such as 5 years, 10 years, 20 years, or even a lifetime. When you annuitize, keep in mind that you receive your annuitization payments with a portion representing your principal and a portion representing the appreciation on which you will be taxed. In other words, you get the added benefit of not paying taxes on the entire distribution—just on the appreciation portion. A 65-year-old person annuitizing a variable annuity could see over 50 percent of the annual annuitization payments coming out as return of principal with taxes being paid on the remaining portion only.

**3. Systematic withdrawal.** The third and least promoted withdrawal program is what I call "systematic withdrawal." With systematic withdrawals, you continue to keep your investment money in the variable annuity mutual funds (as you have since inception), while at the same time retaining the right to withdraw your assets whenever you are ready. You decide the following: (1) when to invest your money; (2) how much of your money to invest; (3) when to withdraw your money; and (4) when to pay taxes and how much.

You can increase or decrease the amount of withdrawals depending on your financial situation, which in turn will determine the amount of tax you will pay at that time. For IRA accounts that hold variable annuities, you must begin taking distributions by age 70½. For personal investments with after-tax dollars invested in variable annuities, some companies will allow you to tax defer your money until age 95. I call this "maximum flexibility."

The best feature of all in the systematic withdrawal plan is the fact that you will be able to tax defer your money until you choose to withdraw it, given the guidelines mentioned above. More importantly, the systematic withdrawal election is revocable at any time; you may decide to lump sum your money out or annuitize at the time of your choosing. Annuitizing, on the other hand, is an irrevocable process that cannot be switched. The bottom line is:

1. Take lump-sum distributions and pay taxes.
2. Annuitize over your lifetime and tax defer.
3. Choose systematic withdrawal for greatest flexibility.
4. Gift the assets to your heirs or to charity.

## The Top 10 Variable Annuity Choices

| | | | |
|---|---|---|---|
| 1. American Skandia | 800-752-6342 | 6. Western Reserve Life | 800-851-9777 |
| 2. Vanguard | 800-662-7447 | 7. T Rowe Price | 800-469-6587 |
| 3. Best of America | 800-321-6064 | 8. Pacific Mutual | 800-722-2333 |
| 4. Hartford Director | 800-862-6668 | 9. Aetna Marathon Plus | 800-525-4225 |
| 5. Equitable | 888-656-8326 | 10. Manulife | 800-827-4546 |

## WHAT IS VARIABLE LIFE INSURANCE WITH INVESTMENT FUNDS?

In order to accomplish our objective of tax-deferred fund investing, a variable life insurance contract with an AAA-rated company utilizing Internal Revenue Code sections 72 and 7702 can be used to accumulate cash value, tax-deferred, during the life of the policy.

This major benefit stems from the fact that any net premium dollars (after expenses) within the variable life insurance policy remain in the policy to be managed by the funds established by the life insurance company. The dollars will grow tax deferred throughout the life of the policy and, unlike the variable annuity, the cash accumulated within the investment funds can be withdrawn utilizing the borrowing provision within the policy on a tax-free basis.

---

### THE ALMOST PERFECT INVESTMENT
### Can You Ever Get All Three?

1. Tax deductible
2. Tax deferral
3. Tax free

---

The best investment would be one in which you pay absolutely no taxes on the investment returns or withdrawals and, at the same time, take a tax deduction on your original investment. The fact is, the United States government, as well as many individual states, is running a budget deficit. Therefore, this type of investment is wishful thinking and we can almost guarantee ourselves that it will never be available.

As a matter of fact, in almost every year of the last decade, Congress has enacted major new laws impacting qualified retirement plans that further restrict your tax benefits and increase your taxable revenue to the government.

Most recently, we have seen many qualified retirement plan contribution limits squeezed further, lowering the maximum contribution from 15 percent of salary or $30,000 down to 15 percent of salary to a maximum of $22,500. At the same time, federal and state income taxes have escalated, putting an even greater burden on the individual to create retirement freedom without major help from qualified retirement plans and Social Security.

Why did you buy life insurance and bet that you are going to die . . . when the life insurance company is betting that you are going to live?

### Variable Life Insurance—How Does It Really Work?

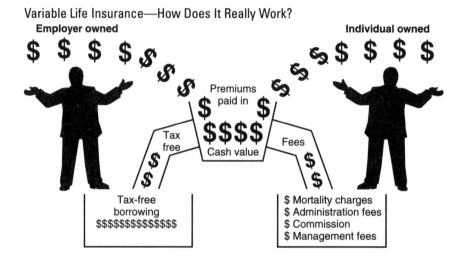

When you pay premiums into a life insurance contract, you have an account with the life insurance company just like you do with any other institution such as your local bank, brokerage firm, or retirement account. You get a statement on a quarterly basis that shows your balance at the beginning of the prior period, any appreciation or depreciation of your assets, and your ending balance. At the same time, it also will show you the allocation of your assets between the different mutual funds and the current value for each fund. What most people fail to realize is that this is *your* account. This is your money, not the property of the insurance company.

The process works like this:

1. You pay premiums into a life insurance policy.
2. Picture your policy as a bucket, where the cash has accumulated prior to paying fees or making distributions.
3. If you paid $1,000 in premiums during the year, the insurance company would then deduct the fees, charges, and so on. The remaining dollars would be invested on a tax-deferred basis.
4. Now, with typical whole life insurance or universal life insurance policies, your life insurance company invests those dollars

in a very conservative portfolio currently paying approximately 7.25 percent.

5. If you choose variable life insurance, then you think that your selection of mutual funds can do a better job than the life insurance company's conservative investment portfolios.

6. Some insurance companies will allow you the option of up to 22 mutual funds from eight different mutual fund families, tax-free switching, and no up-front loads or sales charges on the funds. (However, there could be up-front loads on the insurance.)

7 Cash accumulates in mutual funds within your policy. In later years, you use the borrowing provision within the policy: You borrow your money at rates as low as ¼ of 1 percent—and possibly even a net zero cost borrowing charge—instead of paying capital gains or ordinary income taxes up to 39.6 percent.

## FOUR-IN-ONE BENEFITS

- Do you own no-load mutual funds?
- Has your mutual fund company called you up recently and told you that you can now buy its mutual funds and tax defer any interest, dividends, or capital gains for 10, 20, 30, or 40 years or possibly even forever?

If your answer to these questions is "no," you could possibly be throwing away tens of thousands of your hard-earned dollars.

Receive all of the following benefits in one package. Now, with *one* program, you can eliminate some of your term insurance, supplement your retirement programs, accumulate dollars in a tax-deferred environment, and profit from some of the top no-load fund families available—some of which you may currently own on a taxable basis. You also receive the added feature of a tax-free death benefit payable to your family and heirs.

## SO ADD UP THE ADVANTAGES

- Your policy requires no IRS approval; it is completely selective.
- It allows your money to grow free from income tax within the insurance contract.

- It allows tax-free exchanges between mutual funds.
- It provides tax-free income at retirement via withdrawals and loans.
- Under current taxation, the entire account is never subject to income tax and is not subject to any penalties, unlike IRAs, profit-sharing plans, and other related qualified retirement plans.
- Upon death of the insured, the death benefit is payable to the beneficiary, income tax–free.

## WHAT ARE THE NEGATIVES TO THIS PROGRAM?

A life insurance contract is a contract between the owner of the policy and the insurance company. The policy owner pays premium dollars in return for the promise by the life insurance company to pay a death benefit upon the insured's death. In the early years of the contract, for example, a 35-year-old male pays $10,000 of premium in the first year with a death benefit of $500,000. In the event of the insured's untimely death in year one, the insurance company must pay the beneficiary of the policy $500,000. Now keep in mind, the insurance company is trying to operate a profitable business just like any other company and will book a loss on that transaction of $500,000 plus expenses, less the $10,000 premium paid in by the owner of the policy.

As you can see, the insurance company has a lot of money at risk in the early years of the policy that will decline in the later years once the ongoing premiums paid in by the policy owner, plus appreciation of the mutual funds, take effect. For example, if in later years the policy owner's cash value (premiums less expenses plus mutual fund appreciation) has grown to $200,000 and the death benefit is $500,000, notice that the assets at risk by the insurance company are only $300,000 ($500,000 death benefit minus $200,000 of cash value in the policy).

Therefore, in the early years of the variable life insurance contract, the insurance company will amortize some of its risks and commissions out of the policy. This will be reflected in the reduction of the policy owner's cash value and surrender value; in other words, this is the cost of doing business. Once break-even is achieved in the early years of the contract, the policyholder is then able to take advantage of the substantial tax-free compounding with the investment funds as well as the tax-free borrowing privileges in the later years. Beware of hefty expense- and commission-loaded products that extend this break-even to as high as 10 years or more.

If you are a short-term investor, you have absolutely no business being involved in this type of policy or in any other type of investment that ties up your money, such as an IRA or a pension plan. Short-term investors should look for very liquid investments that they can get out of on short notice, without fees for penalty. This policy is for long-term policyholders, who believe in the long-term benefits of investing in the stock market and have a need for insurance.

## DIVERSIFICATION

Diversification is the key to successful investing. In 10, 20, 30, or even 40 years from now, the government will continue to reshuffle tax benefits and institute changes that will have the potential to severely alter the investments you currently own or will purchase during your lifetime. Diversify across a select group of alternatives that will allow you to have: (1) investments that provide liquidity on short-term notice; (2) tax deductions whenever it makes sense economically; and (3) tax deferral for investments with a long-term investment horizon. As you can see in the accompanying table, we have compared a taxable stock trading account with a joint and survivor variable life insurance policy with mutual funds. The results are both compelling and thought-provoking; hopefully they will inspire you to substantially change the way you invest from this day forward.

### Diversification Made Simple
$15,000 per Year for 30 Years @ 11%

|  | Stock Trading after Tax* | Joint & Survivor*** Variable Life Policy |
|---|---|---|
| Value (20 years) | $635,034 | $783,478 |
| Value (30 years) | $1,432,646 | $1,940,915 |
| Annual Income | $165,414 gross** | $1.2–$7.3 million in life insurance |
| @ 10% after tax | $105,864 after tax | $152,513 tax free (15 years) |

Note: Husband age: 35; Wife age: 28.

* 33 percent tax bracket and 1 percent annual fee deducted from return

** Annual income at 8 percent taxable at 36 percent bracket

*** See a professional life insurance expert who specializes in this area of expertise. Tax guidelines, premium payments, mortality costs, fees, and the strength of the insurance company all play a major role in the long-term performance of these policies. Results are not guaranteed and will vary. Seek help before purchasing a policy and review all footnotes to the illustrations you are presented with your advisors.

## FINAL STRATEGIES

Some final strategies to keep in mind are:

- Variable life insurance can be purchased on one life where insurance coverage is needed and tax-deferred investing is a priority.

- Insurance companies rate your policy, which increases costs and reduces your cash accumulations if there are any health irregularities with the insured. *Solution:* insure the life of your child, spouse, or other family member, while remaining the owner of the policy.

- If you have ever wanted to solve your 37 percent–55 percent estate tax problems (see Strategy #15), consider buying a joint and survivor variable life insurance policy. *This policy insures two lives instead of one and pays the death benefit after the second death—when estate taxes are due.* Use this policy to accumulate cash during your lifetime, pull out as much cash as possible in your later years, and gift the remaining policy to your heirs to help defer estate taxes.

# Strategy #9: Invest in Financial Vehicles that Minimize Risk and Maximize Returns

*The management of your own money may be the most important business you ever operate.*

Up to this point, we've learned that you can build your money up to 300 percent faster through tax deferral, increase your money 200 percent faster by adding a SEP–IRA account, and turn your home into a cash-generating, tax-deductible money machine. With the ultimate goal of achieving total financial freedom, it only stands to reason that you need to become a student of the game of money.

In this chapter, it's vitally important that you develop a simple understanding of how and why money moves create both profits and losses. You've already learned that you're the machine that creates the money. The general idea is to invest that money so effectively that you can live off the income from your investments and ultimately replace your income. At this point, you'll achieve *ultimate leverage.*

Pay close attention as I develop three metaphors that will give you a quick understanding of how money moves. Then, I'll follow up with strategies that will allow you to maximize the use of your investment dollars utilizing both traditional and nontraditional methods in order to speed you to your goal of total financial freedom sooner than you ever imagined.

The first of the three metaphors I'm about to describe is called the circular flow of money. To understand the circular flow of money, see the illustration below:

### The Circular Flow of Money

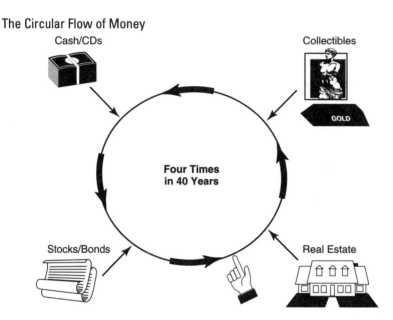

Understand the basic principle that money has no loyalty; rather, it seeks its best employment. What that means, plain and simple, is that there is no emotion or time to money and that it will generally move in a set pattern. If you start in the upper left-hand corner of the circle, you'll see that money is in cash. When money is in cash, it is in the safest location because people are scared. When people are scared, there usually is a particular reason economically. Generally, interest rates are very high, similar to where they were in the early 80s when CDs were paying approximately 10 percent. Why take the risk of putting your money in stocks, mutual funds, or other risk investments when your CDs are paying well?

As the fear subsides and interest rates begin to decline, money will begin to follow the counterclockwise movement of the circle. When interest rates decline, money moves from conservative cash into stocks, which generally heat up during the decline. The ripple effect is quite simple. Companies can refinance debt and acquire new debt for expansion at lower interest rates by creating bigger profits. The general public can refinance home debt from extremely high rates to much cheaper lower rates and put the billions of dollars' difference directly in their pockets, which they will use to go out and buy additional goods and services. This pours more money back into the economy, creating bigger profits at retail outlets, requiring companies to manufacture replacement goods and services, and generally increasing profitability throughout the entire system.

Now let's follow our circular flow of money as it continues to move counterclockwise around the bottom of the circle. Historically, what's taken place as interest rates have come down and markets have heated up is that the Federal Reserve becomes increasingly concerned that growth will get out of hand. Because there are so many dollars chasing a shortened supply of goods and services, retailers have the ability to increase prices to satisfy increased demand. With so much money in the economy, the Federal Reserve usually reacts in a knee-jerk fashion and increases interest rates to try to dampen the economy. This increases inflation, slows the stock market, causes sales to decline, increases expenses, and decreases earnings.

During the initial rise in interest rates, you'll see inflation. As we all know, as inflation increases, the value of real estate tends to increase and, along with it, the stock market rises. Eventually, the stock market begins to decline as investors shun stocks for other investments that will provide a better return.

We now see ourselves on the right-hand side of our circle moving in a counterclockwise fashion. Inflation continues to rage on and the public becomes very scared as people's outlook declines. The bubble is about to break and only the ignorant and high-risk players are left in real estate and stocks. The public gets scared and moves its assets and investments to collectibles such as gold, art, automobiles, and various other items that it believes will hold their value as tangible, hands-on assets. In the height of true hysteria, money moves back again over the top of the circle to cash, in the form of money market accounts, certificates of deposit, and Treasury bonds. Interest rates are high and therefore people are encouraged to place their money in these investments, which are now paying somewhere between 9–15 percent, rather than in any of the risk categories.

## CHOOSE YOUR WEAPON

It doesn't take Albert Einstein to figure out that if you're going to invest your money for maximum return, you should first understand how different asset classes have performed in prior years. Historically, if we study the best-performing assets and understand the circular flow of money, we should be able to duplicate that position for profit in the future. As always, past performance is no guarantee of future results, but it's a heck of a lot better than shooting from the hip.

Stocks have consistently performed better over a period of time; it only makes sense to become a student of stocks. To better understand how stocks operate, let's take a closer look at the value of the big company stocks (stocks with a market value of $300 million or more), small company stocks (companies with a market value of less than $300 million), and various types of bonds, as well as inflation. This will allow us to fine-tune our focus more clearly and locate the best-performing asset classes.

## STOCKS BUILD WEALTH

Always protect your assets' purchasing power. Compare the value of $1 invested from 1926 to 1995 minus the effects of inflation and you become keenly aware of the bottom line. Between 1926 and 1995, $1 invested in small company stocks grew $2,900. Take out the inflation of $10 and you have $2,490. Now on the other hand, go over to Treasury bills, which returned $13, and take out our $10 of inflation and you have real spending power of $2. The so-called most conservative investments (i.e., government Treasury bonds) could drive you broke.

The Rest of the Story
Growth of $1 Invested in Each of Six Asset Classes
(1925–1995)

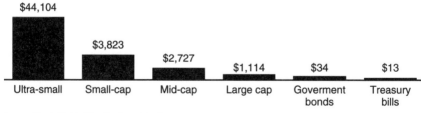

Source: Maggie Topkis, "The Smallest of the Small," *Mutual Funds Magazine*, July 1996.

It's obvious that a combination of small company stocks and large company stocks will provide you with the greatest overall return over a longer period of time. You also should be aware that small company stocks tend to be more volatile than large company stocks, especially during short-term time periods, such as one to five years.

## INTEREST RATES AND BOND PRICES

Not wanting to skip over bonds, let me take a minute to tell you why most people have absolutely no business being in bonds unless they are short-term investors or work with a highly skilled bonds broker. We can see that, over time, bonds provide paltry returns compared to stocks, but the accompanying figure illustrates the severe volatility of bond prices as interest rates move up and down.

Interest Rates and Bond Prices

| Bond Price Volatility (Based on 7.5% coupon) | |
| --- | --- |
| **With a 2% Rise in Rates** | **With a 2% Fall in Rates** |
| 2¹/₂ Years          −4% | +5% |
| 8 Years          −11% | +13% |
| 20 Years     −18% | +24% |

It's obvious that the time to be in longer term bonds (in excess of five years) is when interest rates are falling and you are able to lock in profit as your bond increases in value. In other words, if you purchase an eight-year bond with a 7.5 percent coupon and interest rates fall 2 percent, you will have received an approximate 13 percent capital gain on the underlying value of your bond. Add those two numbers together at the year end if the prices hold, and you'll have a 20.5 percent total rate of return. Total return equals your 7.5 percent interest or coupon plus your 13 percent capital gain.

If on the other hand you fail to sell when interest rates are down and interest rates begin to pick back up, you will give back part of your gain and could ultimately lose part of your principal as interest rates rise. Therefore, my suggestion is, if you decide to invest in bonds, then you should either utilize the expertise of a bond trader or—if you absolutely don't care what happens in between the time you buy your bonds and the time they mature—just buckle your seat belt and hold on for the ride. If you buy a bond with a 10-year maturity paying 7.5 percent and hold it for the entire 10-year period of time and the company remains solvent and in business, you will get paid (despite any volatility), your original principal plus 7.5 percent per year.

## STOCKS OR MUTUAL FUNDS

With all signs of successful investing pointing to the asset category of stocks, we have two choices: purchase stock individually, or purchase mutual fund shares and let someone else pick the stocks.

Don't sabotage yourself; understand that you must have a time horizon. A time horizon is the time in which you hold your stocks to minimize your risk and maximize your return. In our prior illustrations, you've seen the power of stock performance over time. The next question is, How long do you hold these stocks to give you the greatest chance for success? You can't go out and invest in Motorola tomorrow and sell six months later when you see the stock drop 2 points. The following volatility illustration for small company stocks will demonstrate that, the longer you hold your small company stocks, the more your risk diminishes.

### Small Cap Growth Stocks Offer the World's Greatest Profit Potential

Stocks are a great vehicle for the right investor, both domestically and abroad. Remember that today's emerging industries will be the success stories of tomorrow. The goal is to achieve high returns, in which case small cap stocks historically have been the best-performing traditional asset class. The best opportunities for long-term stellar performance are rooted in change. As technological breakthroughs send the profits of small companies skyrocketing or even create new industries, the potential for superior stock market returns could be the ultimate benefit.

Concentrate on creating and investing your cash in long-term stocks. Continue to monitor the underlying strength of your selections. International Business Machines (IBM) provides a classic example of some of the short-term challenges that will arise in your long-term portfolio goals. IBM is well-known throughout the world and was trading at just over $95 per share in July 1992. The stock began to immediately drop

## Time Volatility

Percentage of Time Stocks Have Had Positive Returns
(For periods ended 12/31/95)

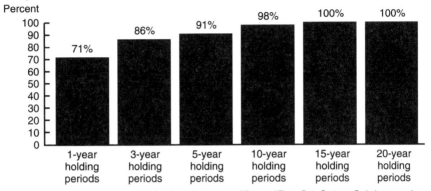

Source: *Kemper Equity Funds Guidebook,* (800)621-1048, source of Data and Tower Data Systems. Period measured: 1928–1995.

based on disappointing earnings, lower sales projections throughout the world, and just plain complacent management in a competitive marketplace. The stock closed below $49 per share in January 1993 and ultimately reached the low $40s in August 1993, before beginning its steep ascent of almost 60 points to $100 per share in the ensuing 12 months to August 1995. The stock hit $121 per share in February 1996, as a result of creating a franchise name of IBM, restructuring management, and reshuffling corporate assets. IBM is now back on track to maintain its leadership position within the computer and technology industry.

The investor has two choices at this point, and I can remember sitting there watching the newspapers and magazines pile on the punishment for IBM as the stock continued to slide during the latter half of 1992. The questions I asked myself were simple, "Is IBM going out of business?" "Is IBM another Bank of America, that wallowed in its good fortune for years and now needs a corporate reshuffling to lean out bloated expenses and increase profitability and focus?" "In this chaos is there a tremendous buying opportunity once the damage is done to the stock?" The answers were pretty simple: No, IBM is not going out of business. Yes, it looks exactly like what happened to Bank of America and many well-known companies and it will probably be reshuffled and as a result build enormous value in its name and its future base of customers and technology. And, yes, it was one of the greatest opportunities ever to realize enormous profits when IBM bounced off of the low $40s in August 1993 and the relative strengths of the company and new investor confidence, based on fundamental changes within the company, drove the stock consistently upward for the next two years. As J. Paul Getty said, "Buy when everybody else is selling and sell when everybody else is buying."

Whether you decide that you would like to pick stocks on your own or enlist the help of a broker, I highly recommend that you take out a piece of paper and create five themes. Use your imagination to project 20 years into the future, look back at the preceding 20 years, and ask yourself, what are the five themes or industries that will not only be around after 20 years but be the leaders of their categories? For instance, we've already discussed industries such as entertainment and satellite television, telecommunications, travel, and the legal system. I suggest that you choose five themes similar to what I've illustrated in the accompanying table and pick five companies under each theme. Based on your investment level, you'll want to own the top one or two in each category and then continue to monitor the remaining stocks under each theme for potential purchase.

## Five Themes of Investing

| 1<br><br>Technology<br>Companies | 2<br>Consumer<br>Products<br>Companies | 3<br><br>Utility<br>Companies | 4<br>Tele-<br>communications<br>Industry | 5<br><br>Special<br>Situations |
|---|---|---|---|---|
| 1. Microsoft<br>(NASDAQ—MSFT) | 1. Procter & Gamble<br>(NYSE—PG) | 1. Southern Co.<br>(NYSE—SO) | 1. Ameritech<br>(NYSE—AIT) | 1. IGT Gaming<br>(AMX—IGT) |
| 2. Intel<br>(NASDAQ—INTL) | 2. Home Depot<br>(NYSE—HD) | 2. NY State Elec<br>(NYSE—NGE) | 2. Telecommu. Inc<br>(AMX—TCI) | 2. Cohen & Steers<br>(NYSE—RFI) |
| 3. Cisco Sys.<br>(NASDAQ—CSCO) | 3. Gillette<br>(NYSE—G) | 3. Texas Utilities<br>(NYSE—TXU) | 3. AT&T<br>(NYSE—T) | 3. Kimco Realty<br>(NYSE—KIM) |
| 4. Hewlett-Packard<br>(NYSE—HWP) | 4. General Electric<br>(NYSE—GE) | 4. Consolidated Edison<br>(NYSE—ED) | 4. Excell<br>(NYSE—ECI) | 4. Recoton<br>(NASDAQ—RCOT) |
| 5. Applied Materials<br>(NASDAQ—AMAT) | 5. Coca-Cola<br>(NYSE—KO) | 5. Northern States Power<br>(NYSE—NSP) | 5. Pacific Telesis<br>(NYSE—TAC) | 5. McDermott Int'l<br>(NYSE—MDR) |

What you've just done is program in your mind the five themes you believe will set the pace for the next 20 years. Interestingly enough, those 20 years also may coincide with your long-term investment goals. If your long-term goal is 10 years, the same concept applies. This is exactly the kind of thinking that could put you in the position to profit handsomely in the years ahead. Time waits for no one, and neither does progress. I think you'll find the themes and strategies that you identify will go a long way toward broadening your thinking about what's taking place in your country and around the world and will help you refocus your investment decisions.

Once you complete your list of 25 names, call your broker and have her send you information on the top two companies in each of your themes. If you don't have a broker and you'd like to do your own research, you simply need to go down to your local library or subscribe to investment publications. Look up the address of the companies on your list and either call or write to the investment relations department to request reports on the company. What you want to do is develop an understanding for at least the first two companies in each of your five themes. You want to track them over time to gain a better understanding of how their stock prices have moved over the last five years. You'll get a quick lesson in how some stocks move in a cyclical pattern, seeming to go down to approximate lows and then rising to new high points.

---

### SAMPLE SOURCES FOR MARKET ANALYSIS AND RESEARCH

1. Value Line Investment Survey (special trial @ $55.00):
   1-800-535-9648 x2729

2. Fidelity Realtime Research Package:
   1-800-544-0003 or http://www.fid-inv.com

3. Morningstar Mutual Fund Software:
   1-800-735-0700, code AWO-AP-GG

4. Standard & Poors Reports on Demand:
   1-800-820-7161

5. Charles Schwab—e-schwab trading and other services:
   1-800-845-1714

---

### INSIDER INFORMATION

If you're not happy getting the funding reports and information from the normal channels and would like to get on the fast track, tap into a computer with access to the World Wide Web to site http://www.sec.gov. You'll now be able to get access to the documents that public companies file with the Securities and Exchange Commission (SEC) for free. These documents will literally give you the fast-track information to what's going on in any company you are interested in before the masses receive it, which could prove vitally important to your success. The detailed information you'll find provides a future outlook as well as any challenges or legal actions against the company currently under investigation. Always log on to EDGAR and click on "search the EDGAR archives." Request information from the 10Ks and 10Qs as well as any proxy statements or Schedules 13-b and 13-g. It may interest you to find out who's buying and selling, as well as who holds more than 5 percent of the voting stock in the company. You may even be lucky enough to find out shareholders' intentions and it may interest you enough to call them up before you buy.

To give you an example of just how invaluable this service can be, when I looked up Geico Corporation, I found out that Geico has entered into a merger agreement with Berkshire Hathaway, Inc., a company owned by internationally recognized investment guru, Warren Buffet. I have just finished reviewing (online) the entire agreement and plan of merger and have printed myself a copy to study in greater detail. The fact that two successful companies and financial guru Warren Buffet are involved has given me a starting place to pursue what could be a potentially rewarding investment. Get online now to get the timely information you need to keep you one step ahead of the average investor.

## ANYONE CAN DO THIS

It doesn't take a genius to figure out a handful of stocks to learn about and own that could ultimately make you wealthy. Follow along as companies like IBM go through a restructuring, first depressing the stock from $80 per share to $40 per share and then moving back up to $110. Or how about researching a company like Merck, one of the largest pharmaceutical companies in the world, with a tremendous pipeline full of new drugs. This is a company that has committed billions of dollars to research and development over the next 10 years and is now creating a major alliance with the managed care industry, which is expected to bloom after health care reforms are put in place. Who would have figured that making network news available 24 hours a day would become a huge success? How about infomercials? Could you have predicted the large number of people willing to listen to 30-minute commercials at 2 AM advertising everything from Abdominal Blasters to dog training, weight reduction programs, and even your own personal astrologer? And, for the life of me, I never figured that we'd be watching funk and bump dancing on MTV or VH1 all night long. You can pick from companies like Nike, with over $1 billion in working capital, to Microsoft, with over $5 billion in cash and up to 25 percent profit margins, to Coca-Cola, which has had returns of over 20 percent per year for the last five years in a row, to the Gap stores, which have the strongest retail name in the nation and are aggressively positioned for expansion. Add to these companies names like General Reinsurance, General Electric, Disney, Motorola, Intel, Home Depot, Automatic Data Processing Systems (ADP), and American International Group, and you have just a few of the companies that allow you to use your tax-advantage dollars to achieve financial freedom up to 500 percent faster.

## DOLLAR COST AVERAGING

You'll hear all different philosophies on investing your money—some that get far out and technical, and others that may even make economic sense. The problem is that the public is demanding an easier system. The illustration you see in the accompanying figure utilizes a systematic approach of very straightforward dollar cost averaging on a monthly basis to average the price of your purchases and give you the greatest chance for investment success.

How Dollar Cost Averaging Works

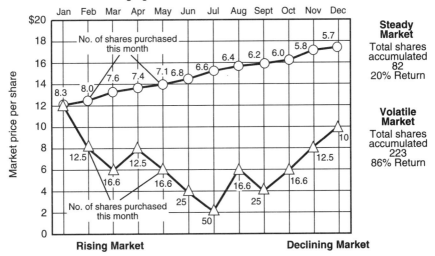

| Amount invested: | $100 per month | Amount invested: | $100 per month |
|---|---|---|---|
| Total invested: | $1,200 | Total invested: | $1,200 |
| Total shares purchased: | 82 | Total shares purchased: | 223 |
| Ending value: | $1,435 | Ending value: | $2,230 |
| Total return: | 20% | Total return: | 86% |

Source: The Enterprise Group.

## How Dollar Cost Averaging Works

It's pretty easy to see in our illustration that when an investor starting out at the beginning of the year in January invests $100 per month for the full 12 months of the year, he stands a better chance of making money using this method regardless of whether the market goes up or down. Please notice that, especially in the down market, he has the greatest chance of loss if he quits his dollar cost averaging program part way through because he's depressed that his purchase has gone down.

Now, follow closely. Let's say you purchase stock at $12 per share in January for $100 that yields 8.3 shares. If you continue to purchase $100 of stock each and every month, you can see that as the price goes up, you receive fewer shares for your $100. That's logical because the price continues to go higher. Traditional thinking would tell you not to purchase the stock at a higher price because you already own it at a lower price. Wrong! As you can see at the end of 12 months, you continue to accumulate shares and, by December 31, you own 82 shares with a total cost of $1,200. Doing the simple arithmetic, you have an ending market value of $1,435 because you continue to average your cost throughout the 12 months. While you have a lower average cost than the ending price per share, you received, in effect, an actual 20 percent return for the year using this method.

Now, let's go back and start with a volatile market. Let's say in January you purchase $100 of a stock or mutual fund at $12 per share, giving you 8.3 shares. Immediately, the stock drops in February to $8 per share and you continue to invest your $100 and receive 12.5 shares. That's almost 50 percent more shares than your original investment. As you follow the volatile market line, you notice the stock literally bottoms out in July at $2 per share. The stock is now trading in excess of 80 percent less than when you purchased it. But you continue to make your $100 purchase and now receive 50 shares of stock, or approximately six times your original purchase. Now, follow our stock along as it continues to inch upward. We all know that you would not continue to buy additional shares unless you were satisfied that something that had taken place in the company would gradually reverse itself and the company would recover. So let's say you're convinced the company is still fundamentally sound and has the people and the marketing plan in place to move forward and grow earnings. By the end of December, the stock is now trading back at $10 per share and you've accumulated 223 shares for your investment of $1,200. Your ending market value is $2,230 and your total return is 86 percent—far outdistancing your steady market program.

## DIVERSIFICATION

Realistically speaking, we know that we are not going to just purchase one mutual fund or stock, but we're going to diversify our portfolio with a variety of investments. Now, keep in mind *ultimate leverage* has everything to do with increasing your chances for success. To take our dollar cost averaging strategy one step further, let's diversify our investments in order to minimize our potential for loss and maximize our potential for gain.

The Power of Diversification

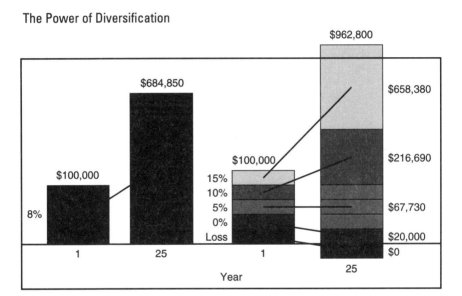

### The Power of Diversification

As you can see in our illustration above, if you invested $100,000 in year one at 8 percent, 25 years later you would have received $684,850. Obviously, this doesn't include taxes and other ravages of inflation. If you took your gross return of 8 percent annually minus your 28 percent tax bracket, you would net 5.7 percent per annum. Now, subtract 4 percent inflation per year and you have a real return of 1.7 percent. It doesn't make sense to be conservative if you care about maintaining your standard of living 25 years from now.

On the right-hand side of our illustration above, you can see how we've diversified our assets into a variety of investments that do incur risk. When you subject your portfolio to risk, you could also incur the risk of loss. Let's look at a severe example, which is extreme from the way I teach people to invest. In my seminars, I suggest people place 70 percent of their money in investments with significant companies (i.e., General Electric, Gillette, Coca-Cola, McDonald's, etc.) to stabilize returns. In our example on the right, you can see we've divided up $100,000 five ways, devoting $20,000 to each investment in year one. Over the 25-year period of time, we've received the following returns for our five investments of $20,000: 15 percent, 10 percent, 5 percent, 0 percent, and our fifth investment of $20,000 lost the entire $20,000. Over the 25-year period of time, our $100,000 grew to $962,800 in spite of only two years of decent returns, two years of absolutely poor returns, and one investment in which we lost the entire $20,000.

## Mutual Funds to the Rescue

We've all seen the proliferation of advertising and marketing material from the over 5,000 mutual funds currently in the marketplace. There are now more mutual funds than stocks listed in the New York Stock Exchange, providing one of the most convenient and affordable ways to participate in the market. Mutual funds pool money from many investors and pursue a variety of objectives, such as small company funds, large company funds, short-term bond funds, long-term bond funds, technology funds, and more.

For choosing mutual funds, I suggest you use a similar process to

Where's Your Risk Tolerance?

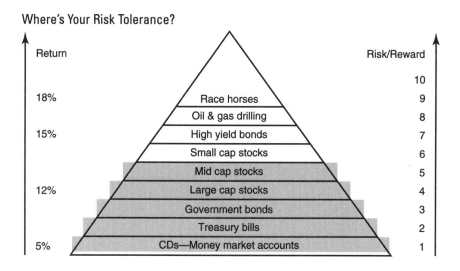

the one that I described for stocks, but break them out into categories instead of themes. Use the illustration below as a guideline and, under each category, consult mutual fund and financial magazines to select the top five mutual funds that you believe will help you meet your goals and objectives with the least amount of risk.

## The Five Categories of Mutual Funds

| 1<br>Small Company<br>Funds | 2<br>Large Company<br>Funds | 3<br>Growth and Income<br>Funds | 4<br>Bond<br>Funds | 5<br>Special<br>Situations |
|---|---|---|---|---|
| 1. Oberweis<br>Emerging Growth<br>1-800-323-6166 | 1. Strong Common<br>Stock<br>1-800-368-3863 | 1. Oppenheimer-A<br>Growth & Income<br>1-800-525-7048 | 1. Salomon High<br>Yield<br>1-800-725-6666 | 1. Portico Retail<br>Special<br>1-800-982-8909 |
| 2. Navellier Aggr.<br>Small Cap<br>1-800-887-8671 | 2. Wash. Mutual Inv.<br>1-800-421-4120 | 2. Fidelity Growth &<br>Income<br>1-800-544-8888 | 2. Pimco Total<br>Return<br>1-800-227-7337 | 2. Robertson<br>Stevens Global<br>Natural Resources<br>1-800-766-3863<br>x137 |
| 3. Portico Microcap<br>1-800-982-8909 | 3. Mutual Beacon<br>1-800-448-3863 | 3. Vista GR & Inc.<br>1-800-648-4782 | 3. Strong Short-<br>Term Bond<br>1-800-368-1030 | 3. T Rowe Price New<br>Asia<br>1-800-638-5660 |
| 4. Third Avenue<br>Value<br>1-800-443-1021 | 4. Janus<br>1-800-525-8893 | 4. Putnam Fund for<br>Growth & Income<br>1-800-225-1581 | 4. Vanguard Muni<br>InterTerm<br>1-800-851-4999 | 4. So-Gen<br>International<br>1-800-628-0252 |
| 5. Landmark<br>SmCapEq<br>1-800-846-5300 | 5. Fidelity<br>Contrafund<br>1-800-544-8888 | 5. Mainstay Conv B<br>1-800-522-4202 | 5. AIM High Yield A<br>1-800-347-1919 | 5. Seligman Global<br>Tech<br>1-800-221-7844 |

Ideally, you'll want to keep your money in a money market account as I've suggested earlier. It acts as your cash reserve account, which also will include check-writing privileges. You will probably have two accounts, one for your personal assets and one for your business assets. Your business assets will stay in the money market account so that you can utilize the check-writing privileges. Your personal assets may begin in the money market account, but then can be dispersed throughout different mutual funds. If you can find a family of mutual funds that you believe can handle your money market account needs, as well as all of your mutual fund needs, then you have found investment nirvana. In this case, you needn't spread your assets over different mutual fund companies, thereby complicating your paperwork when you receive your statements each month. On the other hand, brokerage firms will allow you to have one money market account and invest in literally hundreds of different mutual funds from as many fund families as they represent and issue just one statement. This simplifies your recordkeeping, in addition to giving you access to more than one mutual fund company. Keep your paperwork as simple as possible.

Past performance is no guarantee of future success, but it is one tremendous indication of how things may turn out in the future. Looking back over all the facts and figures and eliminating all the hype and get-rich-quick stories, you'll see how easy it is to strategically plan a highly successful and profitable portfolio with the least amount of risk.

Understanding the circular flow of money, we know that—without a doubt—whatever we purchase will never stay in favor through the entire four cycles of money. We also know that ultra-small caps outperform small caps, which outperform mid-caps, and so forth. If you make an investment based on intelligent selection and research and maintain some sense of understanding of these positions over time, you have a 100 percent chance of success. If you hold those investments in place for five years, you have a 91 percent chance of receiving a positive rate of return; likewise, you have a 98 percent chance over 10 years and a 100 percent chance of receiving a positive rate of return over 15 years or longer.

By subscribing to some of the more popular and effective financial magazines, performing a little Sherlock Holmes research, and tapping into the latest information accessible to you over your computer through the Securities and Exchange Commission Web site, you'll continue to reduce your chances of getting negative returns and sabotaging your future financial freedom. When you finally decide to make some profits, remember: stay within your risk tolerance; tap into market analysis and research; set your time horizon for 15 years; and continue to buy at the point of maximum pessimism and sell at the point of maximum optimism.

## THE NEXT FIVE STRATEGIES—SPECIAL SITUATIONS

Every investor's dream is to gain a slight edge. There is a certain thrill that comes with that phone call in the middle of the night or the excitement of a friend at a cocktail party telling you about something that's supposed to happen within 48 hours. Inside information can totally catapult a stock 10 or 20 points, thus tripling or quadrupling your investment in a very short period of time. A "10 bagger" (10 to 1 return) lives in all of our dreams. The reality is, the uncommon denominator that could give you the slight edge on a consistent basis can only be found through diligent research. We all know about the traditional areas of investing. If you are thoroughly confused by the over 5,000 mutual funds, 10,000 stocks, derivative programs, option systems, hedging strategies, and penny stocks, you'll be relieved to know there are only four categories in which to invest your money.

### Four Classes of Investment

| 1 | 2 | 3 | 4 |
|---|---|---|---|
| **Equity Investment** | **Debt Investment** | **Cash** | **Special Situations** |
| Stocks | Bonds | Money Market | IPOs |
| Real estate | Second mortgages | CDs | |

The equity section includes traditional investments such as common stocks, where you hold an equity share. The debt category includes any investment where you would purchase a debt investment and be paid interest. The third category, cash, is when we want our money absolutely safe, or when we're contemplating where to put it next. Everything else falls into the hybrid category, called special situations. Based on your own personality, your special situation investments will either be the wildest, most hair-brained deals, or more traditional special opportunities that uncover real value and give you real profit potential.

Keep in mind, too, that even a seemingly small 1 percent increase in your return can provide you with tremendous financial advantage and is absolutely worth your time. See the illustration in the accompanying table:

### The Power of Compound Investment Returns

(Assumes an annual contribution of $1,000)
(1% additional return creates a 25% better standard of living)

| Years | 7% Return | 8% Return | Your Advantage |
|-------|-----------|-----------|----------------|
| 15 | $ 26,900 | $ 29,300 | 9% |
| 25 | $ 67,700 | $ 78,950 | 17% |
| 30 | $101,100 | $122,350 | 21% |
| 35 | $147,900 | $186,100 | 25% |

Take as much risk as possible out of your investments before you hand over your money. Get to know as much as you can about the opportunity and how to purchase traditional investments at discounts. As we all know, if you keep doing what everybody else is doing, you get what everybody else is getting . . . mediocrity. Can you ever remember something that the masses did in unison where everybody ended up with exceptional investment returns? Generally speaking, the people who have the edge—those who get in early, ride the wave, and get out before the masses come in—make the most money. The four strategies that follow are devoted to four special situations that will give you that *slight edge,* enhance your returns, and ultimately propel your financial life. We will focus on the following four special situations in the chapters that follow:

1.  Government-backed tax lien certificates that pay up to 50 percent.
2.  The best no-fee stocks, available through dividend reinvestment plans.
3.  Low-cost mutual funds that outperform 85 percent of their peers.
4.  Mutual funds available at a discount.

# Strategy #10: Consider Purchasing Government-Sponsored Tax Lien Certificates

How would you like to take your money that you've invested at 6 percent, hoping to double your investment in 12 years, and instead purchase conservative tax lien certificates, which will increase your yield as much as 400 percent and reduce the time it takes to double your money to four years? Well, that's just exactly what tax lien certificates will do and I'll show you how you can achieve your goals financially up to 400 percent faster using this government-guaranteed monopoly.

Throughout the United States, local governments rely heavily on property taxes to fund their expenses. If people run behind on their property taxes, then it adversely affects the county's ability to operate within its budget. On the other hand, we have property owners who have their own challenges financially, and who are not so much concerned about the county's budget for police, fire, hospitals, welfare, and the like and are more concerned about survival for their families when cash is short. The result is that the local governments create and sell tax lien certificates to the public, as well as investors like you and me.

## KNOWLEDGE IS POWER

Wouldn't you like to know why credit unions and banks purchase tax lien certificates for higher yields? Why registered investment advisors (RIAs) look for conservative but creative methods to increase their clients' yields up to 24 percent? Why you are literally being robbed, holding 4 percent–6 percent low-paying CD rates, when you can increase your yield with tax lien certificates that will allow you to make 16 percent, 18 percent and 24 percent yields?

## Counties and Municipalities Need Cash . . . Now!

Tax lien certificates are created when the county or municipality finds a property owner who does not pay his taxes. The county or municipality will accrue the taxes and penalties for as many years as it takes for the property owner to pay up.

If the property owner turns out to be a deadbeat, the county or municipality will step in and literally sell or option the property off at a tax sale or auction. Obviously, this is the extreme case, and generally what takes place is that the county will issue a tax lien certificate sold at an auction in the state. The certificate is nothing more than a piece of paper that shows the total taxes due on Property XYZ. They obviously need the revenue to run the government, to meet their own expenses.

Just think about any other time you've gotten behind and you've had to borrow money from a friend or relative. The only difference with a tax lien is that the county goes out and finds an investor for you at an auction who will pay the taxes on the property today. The county or municipality sets the interest rate that the investor will accrue, which could be anywhere from 10 percent to 50 percent.

This obviously benefits the county with immediate cash flow and benefits the investor with a low-risk certificate–high-yield interest rate in a tax lien backed by the actual property.

I sat down and discussed tax liens with one of the foremost authorities in the United States today, Ted Thomas, president of the National Tax Lien Alliance. Ted has invested over $100,000 and one thousand hours crisscrossing the country acquiring the knowledge that provides the hidden opportunities in the tax lien arena. His program, "Smart Money Retires Rich," reveals little-known secrets, some of which I'll discuss next.

## The Tax Lien Process

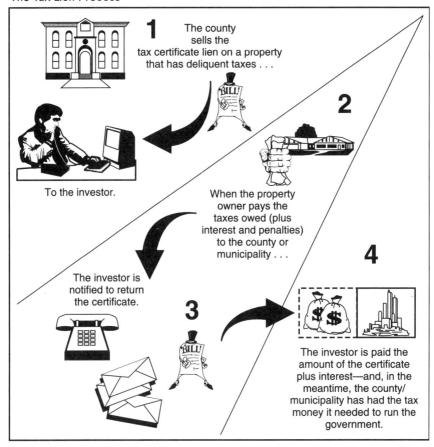

1 The county sells the tax certificate lien on a property that has deliquent taxes . . .

To the investor.

2 When the property owner pays the taxes owed (plus interest and penalties) to the county or municipality . . .

The investor is notified to return the certificate.

3

4 The investor is paid the amount of the certificate plus interest—and, in the meantime, the county/ municipality has had the tax money it needed to run the government.

Source: Reprinted with permission. Ted Thomas, *Smart Money Retires Rich*. For a free report please call The D'Arcangelo Companies at 800-455-3177 or e-mail requests to DARCANGELO@aol.com

Most property taxes are assessed by counties. Since there are more than 3,000 counties in the United States, smart investors learn the rules for the particular county holding the tax sale. The fact that they act independently can be a real competitive advantage in the way that the tax lien process is carried out. The fact is that you can increase your yields up to 400 percent buying government-sponsored tax liens. According to Ted's interviews with county treasurers, he believes that 97 percent of all tax liens are paid off in the first two years. And even in the event the property owner doesn't pay off the lien, you have won the super jackpot. Remember, the tax lien is backed by the property and takes a first place position in front of the mortgage holder as the priority lien. If the property owner does not pay the taxes, the owner will literally lose the real estate for a tiny percentage of what it's worth and the government will help your attorney make the foreclosure.

## Why Don't Property Owners Pay Their Taxes?

There are three general reasons why people don't pay their property taxes, and the first one is as simple as I stated earlier—people run out of money for whatever reason. And we all know people who wait until the last minute to pay their bills, which is the second reason. Third, people die and no one pays the tax until a later date or when the estate is settled. Even more interesting is the fact that you can buy as many tax lien certificates as your finances allow, and you never have to deal with brokers or intermediaries. You deal directly with the government agency. When it comes time to cash in your tax lien certificate because the property owner has now paid the taxes plus interest and penalties, the government will contact you and, upon receipt of your certificate, send you a government check.

## Buyer Beware!

The associated risks in purchasing tax lien certificates can turn ugly if the collateral—the actual real estate—for your tax lien certificate to the government has a value lower than the taxes. Obviously, these are extreme cases, and most real estate is worth significantly more than the taxes. You also can run into trouble if you purchase a tax lien certificate on a piece of property that has been damaged by fire, sits on stilts in a swamp, or has been recently destroyed by a hurricane. The real side of the story is that these properties are easily identified with a minor amount of research. Assessors recognize that properties do vary in quality and they appraise the property accordingly. Keep in mind that property taxes are determined as a percentage of the total property value. If you have a poor piece of property, it's only safe to say that you will most likely have a low property tax. Most importantly, investors can bid on properties with higher tax lien values, translating into high property values.

Last but not least, if you are buying commercial property, do some heads-up research at the city/county public records file and find out where the property is located, who its previous owner was, and what the property was used for. You want to eliminate exposure to any toxic waste on the commercial side of purchasing and, to ensure that your purchases are even more iron-clad, you may want to restrict your investments to residential real estate.

## THIRTY-FIVE TIMES MORE MONEY THAN THE BANK

If you invested in an Arizona tax lien certificate paying 16 percent, at the end of 20 years, your $2,000 investment would grow to more than $30,000. That's 35 times more money than you would have received for your $2,000 IRA contribution invested in CDs. I want you to understand the power of education and how, when county/municipality tax lien certificate rates vary throughout the country, you create even more financial leverage. Iowa tax lien certificates pay 24 percent. That same $2,000 would now turn into $120,000 in 20 years and, remember, that's if you never invested another dime.

The truth is that by not taking advantage of such an obvious opportunity, you could lose potentially $100,000 over the next 20 years. Get a free report on tax lien certificate opportunities by calling our office at (800) 455-3177 and requesting the report from my company.

# Strategy #11: Take Advantage of Dividend Reinvestment Plans (DRIPs)

Everybody loves a discount. One of the biggest discounts you'll ever receive in the investment community is buying stock directly from the issuer company in a program called dividend reinvestment plans (DRIPs). This is a process by which companies can sell already existing shareholders shares of their stock without going through brokers.

Fueling the drive to no-load stock was the regulatory change made by the Securities and Exchange Commission (SEC) in December 1994. This regulatory change eased the stringent rules that had previously made it extremely difficult and costly for companies to get approval for their no-load plans.

To become a DRIP member, you must already own at least one share of the company stock. And, if you are buying a small dollar amount of stock, it means going through a broker and paying the corresponding commission. On the other hand, newsletters such as *The Moneypaper*[1] will help subscribers not only purchase their initial shares without the cor-

---

1. *The Moneypaper,* 1-800-388-9993, ext. 301, 1010 Mamaroneck Avenue, Mamaroneck, NY 10543.

responding brokerage commissions but also will provide educational and information sources to help you build a world-class portfolio.

Once you own one share of a company's stock, call the shareholder relations department to enroll in the DRIP program. Or, if you use *The Moneypaper*'s service, it will handle not only acquiring the first share, but also getting it registered in your name and opening the DRIP account for you. When you dig deeper and look at the real benefits of DRIPs, what you find out is, they not only allow you to bypass brokerage commissions, but they also allow you to reinvest your dividends into additional shares of stock without paying commissions. In other words, all of your new purchases, plus your reinvested dividends, are invested without commissions or fees. Some companies charge a very small service charge, but nothing compared to a brokerage commission.

### Increase Your Returns to 52.5 Percent

A $10,000 Investment for 10 Years with an 8 Percent Dividend

| Reinvest | Without Reinvestment |
|---|---|
| $10,000 | $10,000 |
| With 8% reinvested dividends | 8% dividend not reinvested |
| $12,196 (10 Year Value) | $8,000 (10-Year Value) |

52.5% increase or a $4,196 advantage reinvesting

($12,196 − $8,000 = $4,196)

As you can see, when you reinvest dividends over a 10-year period of time, your money continues to make money, producing a 52.5 percent increase at the end of 10 years. Now, pay particular attention to the advantages you receive with this strategy on purchases and commissions.

Now, let me take you one step further. The enticements get even better because a variety of over 1,000 companies will allow you to invest from $10 up to $250,000 without commissions, reinvest dividends without commissions or brokerage fees, and in some cases, even allow you to purchase additional shares of stock at a 3 percent–5 percent discount from the trading value.

The benefits I've described above will provide you with the following advantage: Commission-free money multiplies faster.

$$\begin{array}{r} 3\% \text{ savings on commission charges} \\ + \ 3\% \text{ discount on DRIP purchase[2]} \\ \hline 6\% \text{ total discount the first day of purchase} \end{array}$$

2. Not all companies offer purchase discounts.

As you can see in the equation above, when you purchase your no-fee stocks, you'll save approximately 3 percent on trading commissions and, at some companies, an additional 3 percent–5 percent discount purchasing stock shares. To dramatize the point, think about this: the average person leaves his money in a money market account for 12 months and only receives a 4 percent to 6 percent money market rate of return. In our illustration, you can use the DRIP program to save up to 6 percent from day one, not including any other benefits.

## WORLD CLASS PORTFOLIOS

The investor guide to dividend reinvestment plans that I obtained from *The Moneypaper* allows me to go through and look up every company with a dividend reinvestment plan and see what the minimum and maximum investments are for each company. But, even more important, let's look at the world-class portfolio that can be developed for as little as $100 per month. This is extremely important because the average person may not think it makes sense to invest a small amount of money or may not believe it's possible to go out and purchase IBM stock at $110 when you can't even buy one share. Over 150 DRIP companies accept minimum investments of $10 per month or more, allowing you to assemble a world-class portfolio of 10 stocks each month for only $100. When investing small amounts of money, make sure that the company plan charges no fee.

---

### TEN WORLD-CLASS COMPANIES FOR $100 PER MONTH ($10 each)

| | |
|---|---|
| **1.** Abbott Labs | **6.** Quaker Oats |
| **2.** Black & Decker | **7.** Newell |
| **3.** Eastman Kodak | **8.** Sara Lee |
| **4.** General Mills | **9.** 3M |
| **5.** Ingersoll Rand | **10.** Warner-Lambert |

Source: Vita Nelson, *The Moneypaper,* special report titled "How to Invest Directly in America's Top Companies and Avoid Brokers," 1993.

---

## MILLIONAIRE INVESTOR'S PORTFOLIO

You'll find that some companies set maximum amounts per month, but you'll also find that at least 90 firms allow you to invest $5,000 per month or $60,000 per year, per company. Some even allow investments as high as $120,000 per year, and you'll find a few that are unlimited.

---

**MILLIONAIRE'S PORTFOLIO**

| | |
|---|---|
| **1.** AT&T | **9.** General Electric |
| **2.** Browning Ferris | **10.** International Paper |
| **3.** Chrysler | **11.** McDonalds |
| **4.** Coca-Cola | **12.** Pfizer |
| **5.** Colgate-Palmolive | **13.** Ryder |
| **6.** John Deere | **14.** Smith, Kline, Beecham |
| **7.** Exxon | **15.** Whitman |
| **8.** Florida Progress | **16.** Zero Corporation |

---

The millionaire's portfolio in the accompanying box would be worth $1,907,000 at the end of 12 months with shares of 16 of the highest-quality companies in the world. Not only that, but her savings on brokerage commissions would be approximately $30,000.

Memberships in organizations and publications like *The Moneypaper* will reduce your paperwork, provide you with ongoing research, and offer buy-and-sell signals for the stocks that you own. They'll tell you when they think there are companies on the DRIP program that are undervalued and allow you to enhance your portfolio's potential returns even more. *In an ideal situation, you could find an undervalued company, trading at 10 percent below market value, purchase shares at a 3 percent to 5 percent discount plus no commission using the DRIP plan, and gain a slight edge of approximately 16 percent the day you purchase the stock.* As always, there are no guarantees that you will get rich quick and the value of your investment will be based on your willingness to get involved. The following is a list of a few companies to help get you focused and started on your quest for dividend reinvestment.

### Information So You Can Take Action

| | | | |
|---|---|---|---|
| Coca-Cola | 1-800-446-2617 | Exxon Corporation | 1-800-648-9291 |
| General Electric | 1-800-786-2543 | Mobil Oil | 1-800-252-1800 |
| Texaco | 1-800-283-9785 | CPC International | 1-800-272-6360 |
| U.S.West | 1-800-537-0222 | Chubb Corporation | 1-800-808-2233 |
| Dial | 1-800-453-2235 | Gillette | 1-800-730-4001 |

You'll notice when you call these numbers that some of them are the DRIP plan agents rather than direct representatives of the company. They'll provide you with all the DRIP information you need to do business directly. I recommend you use a service such as *The Moneypaper* at 1-800-451-4999 to provide you with a better background of knowledge, information, and support services. Ask for any special introductory subscription offers it currently may be offering.

# Strategy #12: Invest in Low-Cost Mutual Funds That OutPerform 85 Percent of Their Peers

Almost 20 years ago, Vanguard mutual funds went against popular investing principles and introduced the "First Index Investment Trust." That year was 1976, and the fund is now called the Vanguard Index Trust–500 Portfolio. This is a billion dollar portfolio with an expense ratio of .19 percent and a turnover rate of 6 percent annually. Compare that to the Fidelity Magellan Fund with a sales charge of 3 percent for investor money, an expense ratio almost 500 percent higher at .96 percent, and a turnover ratio that often is 20 times higher. The turnover ratio shows how often a fund buys and sells securities. A ratio of 100 would indicate that the fund replaces its entire portfolio of stocks within a 12-month period of time.

## OUTPERFORMING THE S&P 500

We have just experienced one of the greatest bull markets in stock market history since 1925. Although most mutual funds have made money because of the bull market run, fully 70 percent have not performed as well as the popular Standard & Poor's 500 Index.

## ACTIVE VERSUS PASSIVE MANAGEMENT

Most mutual fund portfolios are actively managed by portfolio managers who buy and sell securities based on their conclusions after studying the raw market data underlying the stocks in their portfolio. An indexed fund, on the other hand, is an approach that does not try to guess the direction of the market but, instead, attempts to match the long-term results of the related index. In other words, an S&P 500 Index fund would be made up of a basket of stocks very similar to the S&P 500 Index, which is used as the performance indicator of how equity funds are performing.

Most equity funds that are supposed to compare themselves to the S&P 500 Index underperform the index and have fees up to 500 percent higher than an index fund. The simple conclusion is that we should all own some index funds. For example, the management fee for the Vanguard S&P 500 Index fund is 0.19 percent. The average management fee for comparable actively managed funds runs from .75 percent to 1.25 percent. Therefore, you can cut your fees up to 500 percent. Index funds allow you to historically outperform traditionally managed funds (where most don't even match the index) and reduce your risk, on the way to meeting your investment and financial goals.

In the accompanying figure, you can see how the index funds compare against traditionally managed mutual funds for the period ending June 30, 1996.

Mutual Funds Outperformed by Their Respective Indexes (1986–1995)

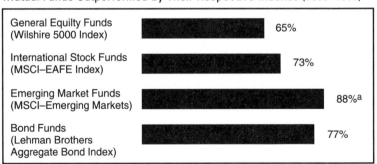

[a] Three years, 1993–1995.

Source: Lipper Analytical Services, Inc. Reprinted from "The Vanguard Group-Index Investing Pamphlet."

## VARIETY REDUCES RISK

A typical S&P 500 Index portfolio consists of stocks chosen from the S&P 500—that means up to 500 stocks that represent the overall movement of the market. Such diversification protects you from the risk that one stock will severely affect your portfolio's returns. On the other hand, you also give up the opportunity for one stock's spectacular performance to substantially alter your portfolio performance. Instead, the index fund historically has provided more consistent performance over time.

Index portfolios now come in a variety of shapes and sizes, beginning with the S&P 500, balanced stock, bond portfolio, international, tax-advantaged, and other related hybrid securities indexes. Some of the companies leading the field in the index arena are as follows:

| Index funds | Numbers |
| --- | --- |
| 1. Dreyfus Mutual Funds | 1-800-645-6561 |
| 2. Fidelity Mutual Funds | 1-800-544-8888 |
| 3. Mainstay Mutual Fund Group | 1-800-522-4202 |
| 4. Vanguard Funds | 1-800-523-1154 |
| 5. Gateway Mutual Funds | 1-800-354-6339 |
| 6. T. Rowe Price Mutual Funds | 1-800-638-5660 |
| 7. Galaxy Funds | 1-800-628-0414 |

Note: This is not meant to be a complete list of index funds, as there are many new additions to the marketplace on a regular basis.

Indexing versus Active Equity Accounts, Long-Term Performance

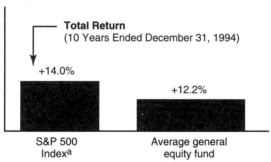

**Total Return**
(10 Years Ended December 31, 1994)

+14.0%

+12.2%

S&P 500 Index[a]    Average general equity fund

[a] The returns of the index have been reduced by 0.3 percent per year to reflect approximate fund costs.

The accompanying figure shows the total return of the S&P 500 Index versus the average stock fund over a 10-year period (ending December 31, 1994). The S&P 500 Index outpaced the annual return of the average general equity fund by 1.8 percentage points. In dollar terms, this return differential equates to a $5,690 difference on a hypothetical $10,000 investment made at the beginning of the period.

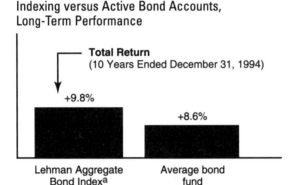

Indexing versus Active Bond Accounts,
Long-Term Performance

**Total Return**
(10 Years Ended December 31, 1994)

+9.8%

+8.6%

Lehman Aggregate
Bond Index[a]

Average bond
fund

[a] The returns of the index have been reduced by 0.2 percent per year to reflect approximate fund costs.

Source: Taken from page 2 of *Vanguard Mutual Fund's Indexing Guide,* titled "Ten Reasons to Index." Vanguard Mutual Funds, 1-800-523-1154.

As shown in the second of the two figures, the Lehman Aggregate Index provided a +1.2 percent return advantage over the average fixed-income fund. In dollar terms, this return differential equals $2,640 on a $10,000 hypothetical investment made at the beginning of the period.

# Strategy #13: Buying Funds at a Discount

The investor seeking the slight edge continually looks for valuable assets or she can purchase at below-market prices. When you went to buy your home, or even your automobile for that matter, did you offer the salesperson the first price he asked? Of course not. And, with some mutual funds, you don't have to accept the first offer either. Pick up a copy of *Barron's* financial newspaper on any Sunday or Monday and turn to the back section after mutual funds and you'll find a caption titled "Closed End Mutual Funds."

Closed-end mutual funds issue a fixed number of shares when they are offered to the public. Thereafter, they trade on the stock exchange (on the over-the-counter market) and are subject to the traditional sentiment of public investors. If $30 million is raised the first day the funds are sold to the public, the capital amount stays constant. They are called "closed end" because you can't call up the mutual fund company to buy more shares, thereby increasing the original investment above $30 million. You must go to the over-the-counter exchange and buy additional shares from willing sellers. In this way, the company stays out of the way and buyers and sellers negotiate the price for which they would like to sell their shares or buy new shares.

## OPPORTUNITY AND ADVERSITY

Traditionally, you'll find that the worst time to invest in a closed-end fund is when it is initially offered to the public because, once you net out the fees for the public offering and related charges, the fund notoriously begins trading below what you bought it for. And you should be leery of funds that go into the marketplace afterwards and raise money from existing shareholders through "rights offerings" or with "enticements to buy additional shares." Simple mathematics suggest such funds could dilute your original investment.

With a fixed number of shares in the marketplace and the public buying and selling based not on underlying market value, you'll find your funds trading at either a premium or a discount to their real value. Once investors come to understand the way this game works, they become completely enthused at the possibilities of buying undervalued assets and thereafter seeing the discount vanish. For example, you find the fund trading at a 10 percent discount, or $9 for $10 worth of value. You do some underlying research and find that the fund is trading under real market value for whatever reason. You believe that value will be narrowed in the future so the fund will trade back in better times at its full market value of $10. If over the next 12 months the fund's discount vanishes, you'll realize an 11 percent return on your original $9 investment. At the same time, if the fund rises an additional 11 percent, you will have racked up a 22 percent return for the year.

## WHERE TO GO FOR HELP

Now, let's take that one step further. In your research, subscribing to publications such as the *Closed End Fund Report,* put out by the *Mutual Fund Forecaster,*[1] you find out that the fund is scheduled to terminate its closed-end status in January of the following year, turning itself into a traditional open-end fund. In this case, the discount is assured to disappear as the fund will be priced to its actual market value based on the value of the stocks in the fund's portfolio at the end of each trading day. The fund listed will be found in the mutual fund section of your newspaper. In this case, you've provided yourself with an additional kicker. The discount disappears, providing you with your 11 percent return on top of the return

---

1. *Mutual Fund Forecaster,* publisher of the *Closed End Fund Report,* (800)442-9000.

that the fund will generate between now and the termination date. This exercise is not just hypothetical, but it is exactly what is expected to take place in January 1997 with a Gemini II Capital Fund managed by the highly regarded mutual fund wizard, John Neff, of the Vanguard Mutual Fund family, who is retiring. By subscribing to magazines and newsletters and doing a little research, you'll be able to uncover opportunities that give you the added advantage to create two profit centers from one investment.

## A LOOK AT THE STATISTICS

In a recent edition of the *Mutual Fund Forecaster,* it took the research of closed-end mutual funds compared to open-end funds one step further by providing the statistics of all closed-end funds purchased between 1981 and 1994.

Average Annual Returns of Alternative Closed-End Fund-Buying Strategies, 1981–1994

| Year | Closed End Funds | Closed Ends at More than 10% Discounts | Closed Ends at More than 25% Discounts |
|------|------|------|------|
| 1981 | + 5% | + 4% | + 4% |
| 1982 | + 42% | + 46% | + 40% |
| 1983 | + 25% | + 42% | + 52% |
| 1984 | + 6% | + 11% | + 13% |
| 1985 | + 22% | + 28% | None |
| 1986 | + 20% | + 29% | + 27% |
| 1987 | − 13% | − 14% | + 4% |
| 1988 | + 18% | − 22% | + 22% |
| 1989 | + 29% | + 35% | + 53% |
| 1990 | − 8% | − 10% | − 18% |
| 1991 | + 39% | + 39% | + 58% |
| 1992 | + 11% | + 16% | + 34% |
| 1993 | + 13% | + 19% | + 27% |
| 1994 | − 9% | − 11% | − 10% |
| Total compounded | + 452% | + 974% | + 1,116% |

Source: *Mutual Fund Forecaster,* February 1996, reprint.

## A Further Refinement

It applied the same 14-year study period to funds selling at discounts of at least 25 percent at the beginning of each year from 1981 to 1994. Not many funds qualified in most years (none in 1985, for example, and only one fund in four other years). With only two losing years (1990 and

1994), a strategy during each year of owning only the funds that began the year at discounts of 25 percent or more produced a total compounded return of 1,116 percent, or 21.2 percent per annum. Of course, with relatively few stocks qualifying in most years, such a strategy has greater-than-average risk.

## CONCLUSION

*Mutual Fund Forecaster* began this analysis by observing that over the period of 1981–1994, garden-variety open-end domestic stock funds provided a 14-year total compounded return of 405 percent. That in itself was an excellent return but, after all, these were generally great bull market years. Most significantly, closed-end funds gave investors an opportunity to significantly beat that return.

First, a strategy of owning all closed-end domestic stock funds every year would have earned 452 percent compounded. Second, a strategy of owning only those closed-end funds that began the year at 10 percent or greater discounts returned 974 percent. Finally, an even more fine-tuned strategy of owning only closed-end funds that began the year at 25 percent or greater discounts returned 1,116 percent—*a 12-fold return.*

Summary: Alternative Buying Strategies

Average Annual Returns (1981–1994)

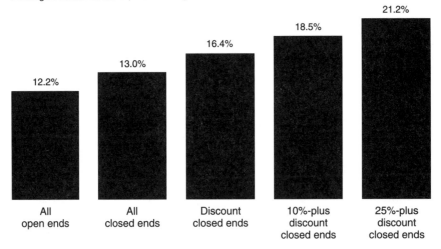

## CAUTION

Needless to say, not all closed-end funds that sell at discounts go up, and not all funds that sell at premiums go down. In fact, most funds move with the general trend of the market—up in bull markets and down in bear markets. On balance, however, during bull markets, funds selling at large discounts go up more than funds selling at large premiums. And, in bear markets, funds selling at large discounts go down less than large-premium funds.

Of course, only diversified portfolios consisting of many closed-end funds can hope to conform closely to the average returns. And the historical results presented in this study may or may not prove to be representative of those that occur in the future. Indeed, since it is unlikely that the next 12 years in the market will be as profitable as the last 12 (which were well above average), we expect the returns earned by all of the strategies discussed here to be somewhat lower. Nevertheless, closed-end funds are an outstanding example of inherent inefficiencies in the marketplace, and they provide investors with rich opportunities for enhancing their portfolio returns.

You must be willing to dig in and seek out opportunities, remaining fully aware of the pitfalls. It's clearly evident that the average investor could reduce risk by buying undervalued assets and have a substantially better chance of striking it rich utilizing the strategies that are enclosed in this chapter versus panning for gold in the High Sierras.

# Strategy #14: A World of Opportunity

---

**TEST YOUR INTERNATIONAL INVESTMENT KNOWLEDGE**

1. Which neighboring country sends the most tourists to the United States each year?

   **a)** Mexico                     **b)** Canada

2. Which country is home to the world's largest bank?

   **a)** U.S.                        **c)** India

   **b)** Germany              **d)** Japan

3. Which country's population owns the most cellular phones (as a percentage of the total population)?

   **a)** Sweden               **d)** U.S.

   **b)** China                  **e)** Indonesia

   **c)** Germany

4. Which company employs the largest workforce?

   **a)** General Motors—U.S.      **d)** AT&T—U.S.

   **b)** Mitsubishi—Japan        **e)** Ford Motors—U.S.

   **c)** Indian Railways—India

Answers: 1. b; 2. d; 3. a; 4. c

The global investment marketplace is poised for rapid economic growth in the next decade and beyond. Just go back in time and think of the world's leading economies that have emerged from developing countries. When I was a child growing up, we used to make fun of products that were labeled "Made in Japan." Well, they are laughing at us now. What if we had the foresight to invest in Japan, Spain, or even China 10 years ago? With the most exciting returns coming out of emerging countries, it becomes increasingly evident that if we can identify established and emerging countries as they move through their growth cycles, we can position ourselves for enormous profits in the years ahead. Pay particular attention to the accompanying graph.

**Emerging Markets Poised for Potential Rapid Growth**

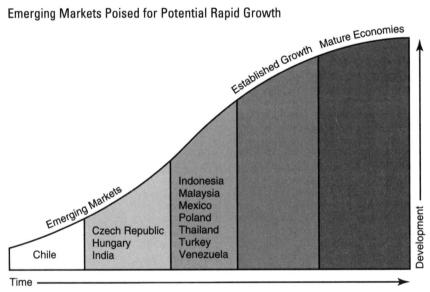

Just imagine Wal-Mart when it broke onto the scene with Sam Walton many years ago. Sam started with a great concept and relative obscurity in small towns throughout the United States. Soon he built revenue and sales based on national acceptance of his plan to get closer to the customer with competitive pricing. As Wal-Mart evolved into one of the megasuccess stories of all time, you can now reflect back and think about how an emerging country also goes through its various growth cycles. First, it starts as an emerging market and then it moves on to sustain itself as an established growth country with communications systems, better utilities, more competitive pricing, higher quality goods, and a stable government. Ultimately, it builds a significant portion of its business for export. Many years later, the economy enters a mature economic phase similar to the economies of the United States, Japan, and the United Kingdom.

One benefit of the massive telecommunications explosion throughout the world is that it has allowed relatively obscure emerging countries to tap into up-to-the-minute worldwide events, information, education, and training. Mass numbers of people who were never exposed to prosperity are rattling the shackles of old world dictatorship and demanding their share of democracy and prosperity. If you're not looking beyond the U.S. borders for investments to play a part in the diversification of your portfolio, then you could be missing out on substantial profit opportunities over the next 10 years. Despite the United States' leadership role in the economic community, the financial unification of Europe, which occurred in 1992, will make the United States the second largest economy in the world. With the globalization of the world's economies and the tremendous growth taking place in the emerging economy of the Pacific Rim, there has never been a better time for investing abroad. Consider these facts:

- More than half the world's gross national product (GNP) is generated by economies outside of North America.

- Approximately 65 percent of the world's total market capitalization lies outside the United States.

- Reviewing all international market performance, no single stock market (including the U.S.) has dominated as the best-performing stock market over time.

- By not diversifying outside of the United States market, you miss over 50 percent of the market opportunities throughout the world.

### World Stock Market Performance for 10 Years Ending in 1994

| 1994 | Finland | + 53 |
|------|---------|------|
| 1993 | Hong Kong | +116 |
| 1992 | Hong Kong | + 32 |
| 1991 | Hong Kong | + 50 |
| 1990 | UK | + 10 |
| 1989 | Austria | +105 |
| 1988 | Belgium | + 55 |
| 1987 | Japan | + 43 |
| 1986 | Spain | +123 |
| 1985 | Austria | +177 |

Source: Morgan Stanley Capital International, December 31, 1994.

United States versus Non-U.S. Market Capitalization

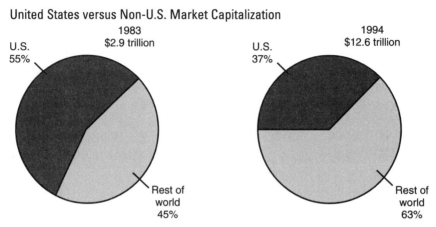

Source: Morgan, Stanley Capital International, *Perspective,* December 1994.

The easiest and most effective means to investing overseas is to invest in either a variety of international equity mutual funds that invest in one country or region or in pure international funds that invest throughout the world with no restrictions. One way to get a better handle on the international scene is to divide up the world market as follows:

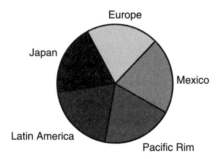

I encourage you to pick up any major international newspaper, such as the *International Herald,* for a totally different view of the markets. You'll also come to realize how other countries interpret our activities. It will broaden your view of world events as well as help you understand how other countries view the U.S. in both the domestic and financial markets. If you keep reading what everybody else is reading, you will follow the herd mentality and get the same results that most other people get, which are generally mediocre.

You can even break countries and regions (i.e., Europe, Asia, etc.) into industries and invest in industry-specific mutual funds. For example:

1. Health care.
   - Mostly nonexistent in many countries, health care opens new markets to established health maintenance and managed care organizations.
   - Pharmaceutical companies play a major role in the testing, manufacturing, and distribution of drugs to new markets.
   - Biotechnology, medical treatment, and technology offer an almost unlimited opportunity for growth and expansion in the health care arena.
2. Infrastructure.
   - Construction, utilities, telecommunications, and transportation are the key industries that will benefit within countries that seek to progress along the growth curve. According to the "World Bank Development Report 1994," road construction has increased 847 percent in South Korea, 453 percent in Indonesia, 219 percent in Brazil, and 134 percent in India in the last 20 years alone.
3. Global natural resources.
   - Precious metals, oil, natural gas, forest products, coal, agricultural products, iron, steel, and the like will be in constant demand as economies expand and countries build more automobiles, planes, farm equipment, and homes; publish magazines and newspapers; and generally increase their economic position.
4. Telecommunications.
   - The information and entertainment revolution is changing the face of world demand for instant access and communication. Privatization of previously state-owned telecommunications industries and deregulation will increase the speed of global growth, bringing both competition and profitability to global communications.

The time is now to develop an understanding of diversification possibilities for your portfolio. As the communication revolution continues to

---

## LABOR, GROWTH, LITERACY AND ENVIRONMENT

If your five themes include industries in each area of the world, look for positive indications in the following four areas:

1. A vast supply of inexpensive labor.
2. Foreign investment that is easily accessible to maintain rapid growth.
3. Rising literacy and education.
4. A regulated and stable stock market environment.

---

South Korea's Infrastructure Projects 1994–1995

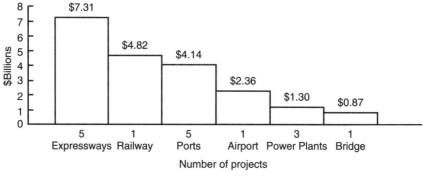

Source: Ministry of Finance and Economy, March 1995.

infiltrate all corners of the globe, emerging market countries are awakening with economic and fiscal growth plans aimed at reducing interest rates, inflation, taxes, and administration. In Asia, for example, factories continue to pop up and governments are turning more progressive. As we develop worldwide diversification, we reap the rewards of massive growth in countries like China, Malaysia, Singapore, and South Korea. The United States economy is expected to grow 2–3 percent, and many countries in the international market will grow as much as 6 percent to 8 percent, annually. International funds can help you balance out the fluctuating performance in your United States portfolio and provide a counterbalance for the ups and downs you are currently experiencing. Just as economies move in different cycles, diversifying your assets across different markets could allow you to maintain a more stable environment for your portfolio.

## THE ODDS ARE IN YOUR FAVOR

In the last four chapters, you've gained a slight edge: the uncommon denominator that separates those who have from those who have not. These special strategies have been designed particularly to give you the added advantage of stepping outside the traditional methods of creating profits and standing at the forefront to gain a sizable advantage.

Are these strategies worth the effort? Absolutely. Understanding these four special situation opportunities could increase your return and thereby speed your journey to financial freedom. The difference between a 2 percentage point increase in returns—10 percent versus 12 percent—on a $30,000 investment for 30 years is $375,315, or 71 percent greater. (Ten percent turns $30,000 after 30 years into $523,482. A 2 percent increase to 12 percent over the same period of time returns $898,797.)

What you've found throughout the last four chapters is that not only are these special situation opportunities effective over time, but some of them require very little expenditure of time. In the trade-off of time versus money, are you willing to spend an extra 60 minutes per week to generate the returns necessary to increase your standard of living for the rest of your life?

### 12 Top International Mutual Fund Management Companies

|     |                           |                |
| --- | ------------------------- | -------------- |
| 1.  | GT Global Funds           | 1-800-548-9995 |
| 2.  | SoGen International        | 1-800-628-0252 |
| 3.  | Templeton International    | 1-800-237-0738 |
| 4.  | Fidelity Funds            | 1-800-544-8888 |
| 5.  | GAM International          | 1-800-426-4685 |
| 6.  | T. Rowe Price             | 1-800-638-5660 |
| 7.  | Vanguard Funds            | 1-800-662-7447 |
| 8.  | Govett                    | 1-800-821-0803 |
| 9.  | Seligman Funds            | 1-800-221-7844 |
| 10. | Scudder Investors         | 1-800-225-2470 |
| 11. | Oakmark International      | 1-800-476-9625 |
| 12. | Prudential                | 1-800-225-1852 |

# Strategy #15: Pass Along a Profitable Family Legacy

If you're still making financial decisions using the trial-and-error method, remember this: "If they taught pilots how to fly by trial and error, we'd all be dead."

| Risks | Business options | Solutions |
|---|---|---|
| 1. Death<br>2. Disability<br>3. Taxes | 1. Sell it<br>2. Liquidate<br>3. Business succession | 1. Estate tax planning<br>2. No planning<br>3. Transfer assets to heirs |

• Bob and Sally Smith mourned the death of their father, who worked so diligently to establish a small chain of laundromats in Boston, Massachusetts. They were looking forward to clearing up their father's legal affairs so they could move back to the Boston area and carry on his business legacy. During probate, their attorney gave them the shocking news: their father hadn't gotten around to having the third witness sign his will. The state of Massachusetts requires three signatures on a will. The judge in their dad's case ended up throwing the will out, assigning an administrator, and forcing the estate into the probate process.

• Malcom Forbes died of a heart attack at age 70 in his Flower

Hills, New Jersey, home. A national icon and leader in the publishing industry with many friends in the financial community, family members of all sides have tried to ascertain the negative impact of the estate tax by projecting it will take $300 million to settle the Forbes estate, which is worth approximately $1 billion.

• Steven and Marti Nagle worked relentlessly in their home-based business, increasing revenues from $40,000 in the first year to $2,000,000 after nine years. In order to finance their growth, the Nagles continued to personally cosign on business loans during early years to start them traveling throughout the United States and Canada and expand their distribution direct-selling group to over 4,000 people. Due to the untimely demise of the savings and loan industry in the early 90s, banks began calling in loans for full payment, sabotaging the Nagles' expansion plan and reducing their monthly cash flow by almost 80 percent. The Nagles were forced to bankrupt their business and the bank pursued the Nagles' personal assets, as they were cosigners on the loan. Personal bankruptcy soon followed.

• Stephanie and Sam Adams took over Stephanie's father's marketing business and employed two of their children, Jason and Matthew. Working 60 hours a week for 16 years, the business had grown to an annual revenue of $1.5 million out of the comfort of their own home.

Business in the future looked tremendously bright, but when Stephanie and Sam recently met with a consultant, he valued their business at $3.5 million. If Stephanie and Sam were to die tomorrow, their personal and business estate would be valued at $5 million and subject to a 55 percent estate tax. After perpetuating their business for three decades and grooming their children to take it to a third generation, the facts remained increasingly clear. In the event of their death, the children, who are the heirs to their estate, would have to come up with approximately $1.5 million in cash to pay the estate taxes within nine months after their parents' deaths. This number would surely use up any cash assets the family had on hand and force their children to sell personal assets as well as the business at whatever sale price they could get.

• Howard and Sandy Friedman run a home-based business in the direct-selling industry. Sandy works as the marketing and financial expert and Howard works as the salesperson. Howard has been taking a salary of approximately $60,000 per year from the business and his wife has been taking approximately $20,000 per year.

Recently they purchased a new home in an upscale neighborhood for $200,000, which they hold as community property, and bought a new Jeep Cherokee with expanded room for the children and the family dog.

One day while flying back from a convention . . . Howard never arrived back home. He died without a will and had failed to file the necessary documents to ensure the financial security of his family. Howard's estate goes immediately to probate and the courts will decide who gets the estate assets. That means the Friedmans' business, home, and assets all will be subject to the whim of the court. Probate fees could be as high as 10 percent and could even include the value of the financed assets.

## THE PROBLEM

If you knew the stock market was going to crash 50 percent two weeks from today, what action would you take with your investment portfolio? Obviously, you would start planning immediately because you have a definite date in mind on which you know a catastrophic event is going to decimate your hard-earned assets. Your goal would be to preserve your money.

The challenge is that, in the United States, we have an estate tax system that, unless you have properly constructed an estate plan, may leave your heirs with legal problems, tax burdens, beneficiaries designated by the state, probate courts evaluating and distributing your assets, legal and administrative fees, and possibly the court deciding upon the guardian for your children, if they are minors.

The fact is the government levies an estate tax of what I call "the cost to exit the United States" upon your death, which begins at 37 percent and escalates to 55 percent and even as high as 60 percent. For example, an estate worth $100,000 growing at 9 percent annually will grow for 15 years to $354,248. A $700,000 estate growing at 9 percent annually will grow to $1.4 million in 8 years and $2.8 million in 16 years. That's two times your money in 8 years and four times your money in 16 years. On the other hand, your estate tax is approximately $37,000 when your estate is valued at $700,000 and then balloons to $320,00 when your estate is valued at $1.4 million. The estate tax balloons to $903,000 when your estate grows to $2.8 million or 26.5 times the original tax, even though your money only grew fourfold.

## THE SOLUTION

The following is a checklist that you should study carefully to put your business and personal affairs in order so that you don't literally throw away the assets that you've worked your lifetime to achieve. The ultimate goal is to pass along family assets and leave a business legacy so that your children or grandchildren can carry on the legacy in the most tax-effective manner possible and keep family assets within the family.

## Vehicles That Affect Your Family's Earnings

The following vehicles affect your family's earnings in different ways.

1. **Last will and testament.** This document states how all property in your name is to be distributed upon your death, names an executor for the estate, and designates a guardian for your children who are minors, as well as a host of other details.

2. **Revocable living trust.** This is simply a document that will allow you to hold title to your assets in the name of the trust. The revocable living trust keeps your estate free from probate and away from others wanting to get involved in your estate upon your death. The term "living" means during your lifetime, you act as the trustor (creator of the trust) responsible for management of the trust assets as well as the beneficiary (the person entitled to receive assets or property during the terms of the trust).

3. **The unified tax credit.** Federal law allows every individual to leave an estate of up to $600,000 (less any transfers subject to gift tax) free of any federal estate tax. If you are married, you also can use the unlimited deduction and transfer up to $600,000 more to your spouse, which would qualify a trust for his or her benefit free of estate tax. If you set it up properly, that means there are no estate taxes on the first $1.2 million of your estate. *Your savings: $192,500.*

Linda and Harry Johnson are successful home-based business entrepreneurs who wouldn't interrupt their busy careers to take the time to do some planning. As we all know, when you're busy in your careers, sometimes you don't exactly dot all your i's and cross all your t's, especially in specific areas where you are not an expert.

Linda and Harry purchased their residence in joint tenancy, which will keep their house out of probate. In the untimely event of Harry's death, the home will not go through the probate process, but all of their other assets will. The widow probably stated where the assets should be distributed, but there is no revocable living trust in place to avoid the probate system. Now the business that they've worked so hard to accumulate during their lifetime and intended to pass along as their family legacy will not only be subject to the probate process but also the entire estate will be subject to taxes on any estate values higher than $600,000. In addition, Linda will have to pay a capital gains tax on one-half of the appreciation of their home.

The revocable living trust becomes an integral part of business succession and planning if your total assets are valued over $600,000. Without a revocable living trust, all of your assets will remain in the owner's name. When you're gone, your heirs must try to figure out how to assume control of the business, write checks, expand the business, or simply take title to it. The problem lies in the fact that, with everything in your name, your heirs will be unable to transfer the title to their name. Why let probate control the future of your business when a revocable living trust will put your business in the hands of those most capable . . . your children, lifetime employees, or your partner?

The challenge is that, once your estate exceeds $1.2 million in as-

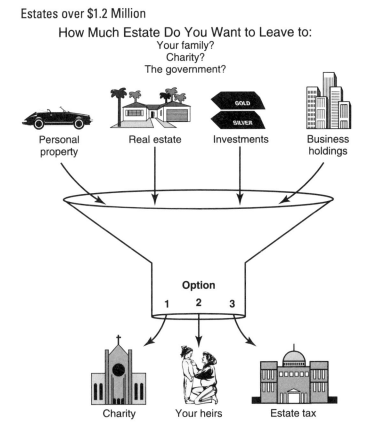

Estates over $1.2 Million

How Much Estate Do You Want to Leave to:
Your family?
Charity?
The government?

Personal property · Real estate · Investments · Business holdings

Option 1 2 3

Charity · Your heirs · Estate tax

sets, you're literally penalized for every dollar you accumulate, in that you will be susceptible to estate taxes beginning at 37 percent and going as high as 53 percent. The accompanying table illustrates the estate tax schedule. You spend a lifetime building your business and your assets. You maximize tax benefits and generate income so that at the end of each year your tax obligations are paid in full. Yet, the day you die, you may owe tens of thousands, or even hundreds of thousands, of dollars in estate taxes on assets over $600,000 for single people and $1.2 million for married couples.

### Estate Tax Rate Schedule

| Size of Estate | Tax |
|---|---|
| $ 3,000,000 | $ 784,000 |
| $ 4,000,000 | $ 1,318,000 |
| $ 5,000,000 | $ 1,868,000 |
| $ 6,000,000 | $ 2,418,000 |
| $ 7,000,000 | $ 2,968,000 |
| $ 8,000,000 | $ 3,518,000 |
| $ 9,000,000 | $ 4,068,000 |
| $10,000,000 | $ 4,618,000 |
| $12,000,000 | $ 5,788,000 |
| $14,000,000 | $ 6,988,000 |
| $16,000,000 | $ 8,188,000 |
| $18,000,000 | $ 9,388,000 |
| $20,000,000 | $10,588,000 |

What we have is a ticking time bomb that will ultimately diminish the value of your business and affect your ability to transfer your business assets to your children or any other family member. At the same time, your business is part of your entire estate, which will be significantly reduced because of estate taxes.

But what if you received the letter on page 171 with an offer from the "Department of the Treasury—Internal Revenue Service" to pay your future estate tax liability off today at pennies on the dollar.

There are three ways by which you can pay off your estate taxes; these are listed below. Your goal is to maximize the value of your estate going to your heirs with a minimum amount of out-of-pocket cash. You've worked your entire life to create your estate. Why not solve your estate tax obligation and pass along your legacy with minimum expense and positive leverage?

**1. The 100 percent method.** Within nine months after the death of both parents, the estate taxes are due. The 100 percent method leaves the

**For Illustrative Purposes Only**

Department of the Treasury
Internal Revenue Service

Dear Taxpayer:

We have been notified that at the death of you and your spouse, your heirs will owe the United States Government the sum of **$1,000,000** in Death Taxes. These taxes are payable in CASH or by MONEY ORDER within **NINE MONTHS** after your demise.

Payment can be made by liquidating assets of your estate or from cash which you have already paid taxes on and saved for your family.

We do, however, offer an alternative installment plan for selected taxpayers. The amount of the installment payment is **$21,688** which represents a **2.17 percent interest rate on the amount due the IRS** and you are required to make this payment for **five years only.** After making the five years of interest payments we will consider your taxes "PAID IN FULL." Furthermore, we guarantee that under this plan **you will never pay more than 10.85 percent of the amount of tax set forth above.**

Should you desire to explore this matter further, the "agent" bearing this letter can more fully explain how this attractive alternative works.

I remain your "Favorite Uncle."

Very Truly Yours,
**UNCLE SAM**
Internal Revenue Service

cc: The Eastman Company, Inc.

Note: This is not an actual IRS letter. This illustration is used to dramatize a point regarding estate tax reduction planning.
Source: Reprint Courtesy of Eastman and Benirschke, San Diego, CA.

heirs to take cash or savings on hand or sell assets from the estate to pay the IRS. The only problem with this method is that if you owe the IRS an amount of money, say $100,000, and you take cash and pay it, then ultimately what you're doing is taking $100,000 cash out of circulation. If instead you kept that $100,000 and invested it in mutual funds and received a 10 percent rate of return over the next 20 years, it would return you $672,750. In other words, it will cost you $572,750 of potential assets to pay $100,000 today.

**2. The 100 percent plus method.** As heirs of the business and estate, you'll notice in running your own business that a lot of times cash assets aren't available to pay immediate obligations. Therefore, you are forced to sell assets in the most untimely markets to raise cash. You liquidate assets at a loss, you mortgage property, or you even go out and borrow money using the assets of the business or assets of the estate as collateral. If you owe the IRS $100,000 and you need to sell assets quickly, then let's estimate that you sell them at a 20 percent discount, so, in other words, you have sold $120,000 worth of market value assets to raise $100,000. You're going to throw away $20,000 for every $100,000 you need to raise. If you borrow money at the rate of 12 percent, then $100,000 will cost you $12,000 a year in interest plus an additional $12,000 that you could be making on the $100,000 if you'd invested it. That's a total of $24,000 per year out of circulation and out the window.

**3. The discounted dollar method.** You can see from the example of the Internal Revenue Service letter that it appears the IRS is making you an offer to discount your future estate obligation and pay that future obligation today at pennies on the dollar. Well, the fact is, the IRS will not allow you to do that. It wants its money nine months after the date of death and not a day later.

The only way you can use this strategy is not through your financial consultant, your stockbroker, your attorney, or your accountant, but through your insurance agent. By utilizing the awesome leverage in life insurance products, properly structured to meet your objectives, you'll be able to save literally tens and hundreds of thousands of dollars. You'll be able to discount (depending on your situation) your estate tax up to 95 percent and lower your effective estate tax bracket from as high as 55 percent to as little as 10 percent.

The process works like this:

**1. $10,000 annual gift per spouse.** During your lifetime, both spouses can gift up to $10,000 each to any number of people they desire. You can use this annual gifting to get money out of the estate.

**2. Irrevocable life insurance trust.** The irrevocable life insurance trust set up by your attorney will create an instant estate that will pay death taxes and guarantee the funds necessary to continue the business and maintain the estate of the deceased. This trust is set up with the heirs as the beneficiary and a designated trustee. Each spouse can gift a maximum $10,000 tax free each year to each child or individual, who in turn can designate the money for deposit into the irrevocable life insurance trust.

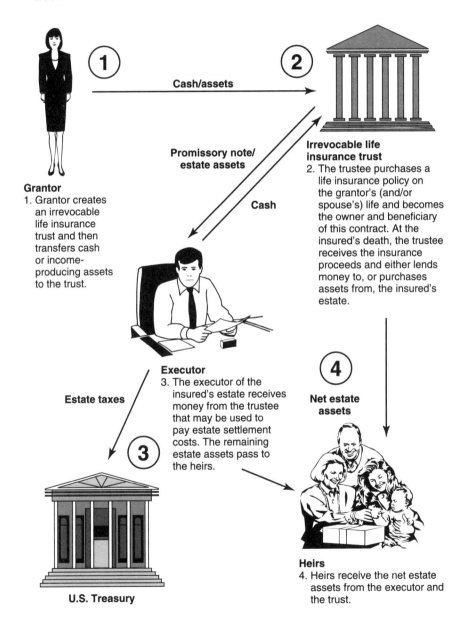

**1**

**Cash/assets**

**2**

**Promissory note/ estate assets**

**Cash**

**Irrevocable life insurance trust**

2. The trustee purchases a life insurance policy on the grantor's (and/or spouse's) life and becomes the owner and beneficiary of this contract. At the insured's death, the trustee receives the insurance proceeds and either lends money to, or purchases assets from, the insured's estate.

**Grantor**

1. Grantor creates an irrevocable life insurance trust and then transfers cash or income-producing assets to the trust.

**Executor**

3. The executor of the insured's estate receives money from the trustee that may be used to pay estate settlement costs. The remaining estate assets pass to the heirs.

**Estate taxes**

**3**

**4**

**Net estate assets**

**Heirs**

4. Heirs receive the net estate assets from the executor and the trust.

**U.S. Treasury**

**3. Life insurance inside the trust.** The trustee of the trust on behalf of the children will purchase a "second-to-die policy" (if there are two spouses) on the parents that will be owned by the trust with the children as the beneficiary. The second-to-die policy can be up to 30 percent cheaper because you're insuring two lives instead of one.

**4. Death of the second parent.** Since the parents have no ownership rights to any of the money in the trust or the policy, then upon their death, the life insurance benefits will pass to the children's estate income tax-free.

If the parents pass away with business and personal assets valued at $3 million and have maximized the marital deduction and unified credit, then they'll pay no taxes on the first $1.2 million of the estate. Taxes on the remaining $1.8 million will be $784,000.

For simplicity, let's assume both parents are 50 years old and the cost of their second-to-die life insurance policy with a $784,000 death benefit costs approximately $20,000 per year, for five years.

Each parent gifts up to $10,000 to a life insurance trust for the benefit of the children. The trustee (your brother-in-law, for example) uses the $20,000 annually to purchase life insurance in the trust for $784,000. In effect, we have solved a $784,000 future debt at $20,000 annually for five years (12.5¢ per $1.00 owed). That's a discount of 87.5 percent.

## Multiply Gifts up to 50 Times

Now that you understand the power of "ultimate leveraging," take my thought process a little further. When grandparents or parents gift money to children into their accounts, why not purchase a life insurance policy with the children as the beneficiary? In other words, if grandparents have assets that they know will garner an estate tax when they pass away, then why not begin gifting assets while they're alive? This will eliminate taxes on their estate and allow the grandparents to take that $10,000 annually, for example, and purchase a life insurance policy on their lives or the life of one of their own children, leaving the grandchildren as the beneficiaries. For example, see the box below.

---

### GRANDPARENT AGE 65 GIFTS $10,000 PER YEAR

$10,000 per year for 20 years buys a $400,000 life insurance policy. It produces 40 times the annual gift or 400 times the 10 years of annual premiums.

---

## Leverage to Charity

Use the same "ultimate leverage" strategies to create massive gifts to the charities of your choice. Charities always need cash. Gift part of your money in cash each year and part of your money in the way of a life insurance policy with the charity as the beneficiary. Young adults who want to donate $2,000 per year to the charity of their choice just as their career is starting to take off can purchase a policy with a value of $50,000 or even $100,000. For example:

- Young adult age 35.
- $2,000 annual premiums for 10 years buys $100,000 death benefit.

As you can see, you have multiplied your gift by 50 times to get a $100,000 future death benefit for your charity. This is a new way for an institution to guarantee the future, by creating $20–$30 million or more in a life insurance endowment. Using some of the concepts learned earlier, parents or grandparents could use the second-to-die life insurance policy (up to 30 percent cheaper to operate than a policy on one person's life) to reduce the cost of the policy or use the savings to buy more life insurance. This tactic will provide even greater leverage to the charity and to the couple creating the gift. Just think of the fanfare you get when you gift $100,000 versus $2,000.

## Family Business Planning

Business owners also should investigate "family limited partnerships." In this case, you're trying to protect yourself from the onslaught of lawsuits as well as transfer assets to family members to lessen the estate tax burden and pass on the family business.

Your assets are transferred to your limited partnership, which is generally set up with your owning 5 percent of the general partnership's interest. The limited partners will own 95 percent of the remaining partnership. You, as the owner of the business, along with your spouse, are the general partner, which means you have the authority and the decision-making power to manage the partnership. Over the years, you want to begin to divest yourself of some of the limited partnership interest to family members (i.e., children or grandchildren) using the $10,000 annual gift per spouse. Or you can even use a portion of your $600,000 unified credit and $600,000 of marital deduction for up to $1.2 million. No one said you had to wait until you die to use the $600,000 unified credit and

$600,000 marital deduction. It makes sense to begin gifting assets out of your estate sooner, so that they will begin appreciating in your children's estates. This also stops the estate tax from accumulating on every new dollar you make at the rate of 37 percent–55 percent.

Over many years, you can continue to gift the bulk of the limited partnership's interest away from yourself and toward your children. These assets are generally safe from creditors and are effective in your estate planning taxes.

You've just created a tremendous asset protection tool as well as a business success plan without the ravaging effects of estate taxes. Just think, if you have a frivolous lawsuit on the horizon and someone comes after the partnership assets, you and your spouse are the general partners. You also hold limited partnership interests with your children, so if a judgment is reached against you, distributions to you as a limited partner can be attached. As a general partner, you have the power to withhold distributions to the limited partners (yourself), thereby stringing out the frivolous lawsuit assignee and potentially settling for pennies on the dollar or forcing the suit to disappear completely.

Estate planning for your business is a subject vital to the perpetuation of your wealth. Each individual case is very personal and yours may include partners, family members, public or private stock, key-person insurance, buy–sell agreements, cross-purchase agreements, stock redemption, and transfer strategies—all of which will work in your favor. Consult a business consultant or life insurance *specialist.* Be smart . . . be intelligent . . . be informed.

# INDEX